SYMBOLIC COMPUTATION

Artificial Intelligence

J. W. Lloyd

Foundations of Logic Programming

John Wylie Lloyd

Department of Computer Science
University of Melbourne
Parkville
Victoria 3052, Australia

ISBN 3-540-13299-6 Springer-Verlag Berlin Heidelberg New York Tokyo
ISBN 0-387-13299-6 Springer-Verlag New York Heidelberg Berlin Tokyo

Library of Congress Cataloging in Publication Data.
Lloyd, J. W. (John Wylie), 1947- Foundations of logic programming. (Symbolic computation. Artificial intelligence) Bibliography: p. Includes Index. 1. Electronic digital computers–Programming. 2. Logic, Symbolic and mathematical. 3. Programming languages (Electronic computers)–Semantics. I. Title. II. Series.
QA76.6.L583 1984 001.64'2 84-20277

Printed in Germany

Printing: Beltz Offsetdruck, Hemsbach/Bergstr.;
Bookbinding: J. Schäffer OHG, Grünstadt
2145/3140-543210

To

Susan, Simon and Patrick

PREFACE

This book gives an account of the mathematical foundations of logic programming. I have attempted to make the book self-contained by including proofs of almost all the results needed. The only prerequisites are some familiarity with a logic programming language, such as PROLOG, and a certain mathematical maturity. For example, the reader should be familiar with induction arguments and be comfortable manipulating logical expressions. Also the last chapter assumes some acquaintance with the elementary aspects of metric spaces, especially properties of continuous mappings and compact spaces.

Chapter 1 presents the declarative aspects of logic programming. This chapter contains the basic material from first order logic and fixpoint theory which will be required. The main concepts discussed here are those of a logic program, model, correct answer substitution and fixpoint. Also the unification algorithm is discussed in some detail.

Chapter 2 is concerned with the procedural semantics of logic programs. The declarative concepts are implemented by means of a specialized form of resolution, called SLD-resolution. The main results of this chapter concern the soundness and completeness of SLD-resolution and the independence of the computation rule. We also discuss the implications of omitting the occur check from PROLOG implementations.

Chapter 3 discusses negation. Current PROLOG systems implement a form of negation by means of the negation as failure rule. The main results of this chapter are the soundness and completeness of the negation as failure rule.

an area of great theoretical importance.

The material of chapters 1 to 3, which is now very well established, could be described as "what every PROLOG programmer should know". In chapter 4, I have allowed myself the luxury of some speculation. I believe the material presented there will eventually be incorporated into a much more extensive theoretical foundation for concurrent PROLOGs. However, this chapter is incomplete insofar as I have confined attention to a single perpetual process. Problems of concurrency and communication, which are not very well understood at the moment, have been ignored.

My view of logic programming has been greatly enriched by discussions with many people over the last three years. In this regard, I would particularly like to thank Keith Clark, Maarten van Emden, Jean-Louis Lassez, Frank McCabe and Lee Naish. Also various people have made suggestions for improvements of earlier drafts of this book. These include Alan Bundy, Hervé Gallaire, Joxan Jaffar, Donald Loveland, Jeffrey Schultz, Marek Sergot and Rodney Topor. To all these people and to others who have contributed in any way at all, may I say thank you.

July 1984 JWL

CONTENTS

Chapter 1. DECLARATIVE SEMANTICS

This chapter presents the declarative semantics of logic programs. After a brief introduction, the basic syntax and terminology of logic programs is introduced. We then discuss interpretations and models of logic programs. These provide the declarative semantics. Then the key concept of a correct answer substitution is introduced. This provides a declarative understanding of the desired output from a program and a goal. The basic fixpoint results are then proved and the chapter culminates with a fixpoint characterization of the least Herbrand model of a program.

§1. INTRODUCTION

Logic programming began in the early 1970's as a direct outgrowth of earlier work in automatic theorem proving and artificial intelligence. Constructing automated deduction systems is, of course, central to the aim of achieving artificial intelligence. Building on work of Herbrand [27] in 1930, there was much activity in theorem proving in the early 1960's by Prawitz [50], Gilmore [22], Davis, Putnam [16] and others. This effort culminated in 1965 with the publication of the landmark paper by Robinson [51], which introduced the resolution rule. Resolution is an inference rule which is particularly well-suited to automation on a computer.

The credit for the introduction of logic programming goes mainly to Kowalski [31] and Colmerauer [15], although Green [23] and Hayes [26] should be mentioned in this regard. In 1972, Kowalski and Colmerauer were led to the fundamental idea that *logic can be used as a programming language.* The acronym PROLOG (PROgramming in LOGic) was conceived and the first PROLOG interpreter [15] was implemented in the language ALGOL-W by influential version written in FORTRAN).

The idea that first order logic, or at least substantial subsets of it, can be used as a programming language was revolutionary, because, until 1972, logic had only ever been used as a specification or declarative language in computer science. However, what [31] shows is that logic has a *procedural interpretation*, which makes it very effective as a programming language. Briefly, a program clause $A \leftarrow B_1,...,B_n$ is regarded as a *procedure definition.* If $\leftarrow C_1,...,C_k$ is a goal clause, then each C_j is regarded as a *procedure call.* A program is run by giving it an initial goal. If the current goal is $\leftarrow C_1,...,C_k$, a step in the computation involves unifying some C_j with the head A of a program clause $A \leftarrow B_1,...,B_n$ and thus reducing the current goal to the goal $\leftarrow (C_1,...,C_{j-1},B_1,...,B_n,C_{j+1},...,C_k)\theta$, where θ is the unifying substitution. Unification thus becomes a uniform mechanism for parameter passing, data selection and data construction. The computation terminates when the empty goal is produced.

One of the most important practical outcomes of the research so far has been the language PROLOG, which is based on the Horn clause subset of logic. The majority of logic programming systems available today are either PROLOG interpreters or compilers. Most use the simple computation rule, which always selects the leftmost atom in a goal. (We call these *standard* PROLOGs). However, logic programming is by no means limited to PROLOG. It is essential not only to find more appropriate computation rules, but also to find ways to program in larger subsets of logic, not just the clausal subset. In particular, such systems need not necessarily be based on resolution. They could be non-clausal systems with many inference rules [7], [24], [25]. This account only discusses logic programming systems based on resolution and concentrates particularly on the PROLOG systems which are currently available.

As we stated above, most logic programming systems are resolution theorem provers. However, it is important to appreciate that they are particularly single-minded and efficient theorem provers. Such systems do not face anything like the computational complexity that a theorem prover in, say, group theory has to contend with. Because of the restriction to Horn clauses and the restrictions on the proof procedure, many logic programs are almost determinate (that is, run with almost no backtracking) and thus support the idea that deduction can be usefully thought of as computation.

One of the main ideas of logic programming, which is due to Kowalski [30], [32], is that an algorithm consists of two disjoint components, the logic and the control. The logic is the statement of *what* the problem is that has to be solved. The control is the statement of *how* it is to be solved. The ideal of logic programming is that the programmer should only have to specify the logic component of an algorithm. The control should be exercised solely by the logic programming system. Unfortunately, this ideal has not yet been achieved with current logic programming systems.

In order to achieve the ideal of logic programming, there are two broad problems which have to be solved. The first of these is the *control problem.* Currently, programmers need to provide a lot of control information, partly by the ordering of clauses and atoms in clauses and partly by extra-logical control features, such as cut. However, these control features are rather unsatisfactory for a number of reasons. The first task in the solution of the control problem will be the provision of more satisfactory control features for the use of programmers. The second task will be the transfer of responsibility for control from the programmer to the system itself.

The second problem is the *negation problem.* The Horn clause subset of logic does not have sufficient expressive power and hence PROLOG systems allow negative literals in the bodies of clauses. However, they do not implement negation, but only a problematic, imperfect version by means of the negation as failure rule. Current research is aimed at a better understanding of the negation as failure rule, as well as finding a replacement which is closer to logical negation.

Logic has two other interpretations. The first of these is the *database interpretation.* Here a logic program is regarded as a database [37], [20], [21]. We thus obtain a very natural and powerful generalization of relational databases, which correspond to logic programs consisting solely of ground unit clauses. The concept of logic as a uniform language for data, programs, queries, views and integrity constraints has great theoretical and practical potential.

The third interpretation of logic is the *process interpretation.* In this processes. A step in the computation is the reduction of a process to a system of processes (the ones that occur in the body of the clause that matched the call). Shared variables act as communication channels between processes. There are now several concurrent PROLOGs based on the process interpretation [11], [12], [54]. This interpretation allows logic to be used for operating system applications and object-oriented programming [55].

It is clear that logic thus provides a single formalism for apparently diverse parts of computer science. Logic provides us with a general-purpose, problem-solving language, a concurrent language suitable for operating systems and also a foundation for database systems. This range of application together with the simplicity, elegance and unifying effect of logic programming assures it of an important and influential future. Logical inference is about to become the fundamental unit of computation.

This view is strongly supported by the Japanese fifth generation computer project [43]. Logic programming has been chosen to provide the core programming language for this very ambitious 10 year project, which aims to produce innovative computer systems for the 1990's. The Japanese hope to build new computer architectures with VLSI to directly support a parallel logic programming language. This will provide a basis for computer systems with expert knowledge, problem-solving ability and access via natural language, speech and so on, which can truly be regarded as intelligent assistants.

§2. LOGIC PROGRAMS

This section introduces the syntax of logic programs. In fact, more generally, we will introduce the syntax of well-formed formulas of a first order theory. While all the requisite concepts from first order logic will be discussed informally in this and subsequent sections, it would be helpful for the reader to have some wider background on logic. We suggest reading the first few chapters of [8], [38], [42] or [56].

First order logic has two aspects: its syntax and its semantics. The syntactic aspect is concerned with well-formed formulas admitted by the grammar of a formal language, as well as deeper proof-theoretic issues. The semantics is concerned with the meanings attached to the symbols in the well-formed formulas. We postpone the discussion of semantics to the next section.

A *first order theory* consists of an alphabet, a first order language, a set of axioms and a set of inference rules [42], [56]. The first order language consists of the well-formed formulas of the theory. The axioms are a designated subset of well-formed formulas. The axioms and rules of inference are used to derive the theorems of the theory. We now proceed to define alphabets and first order languages.

Definition An *alphabet* consists of seven classes of symbols:
(a) variables
(b) constants
(c) functions
(d) predicates
(e) connectives
(f) quantifiers
(g) punctuation symbols

Classes (e) to (g) are the same for every alphabet, while classes (a) to (d) vary from alphabet to alphabet. For any alphabet, only the classes (b) and (c) may be empty. We adopt some informal notational conventions for these classes. Variables will normally be denoted by the letters u, v, w, x, y and z (possibly subscripted). Constants will normally be denoted by the letters a, b and c (possibly subscripted). Functions of various arities > 0 will normally be denoted by the letters f, g and h (possibly subscripted). Predicates of various arities ≥ 0 will normally be denoted by the letters p, q and r (possibly subscripted). Occasionally, it will be convenient not to apply these conventions rigorously. In such a case, possible confusion will be avoided by the context. The connectives are $\sim$, $\wedge$, $\vee$, $\rightarrow$ and $\longleftrightarrow$, while the quantifiers are $\exists$ and $\forall$. Finally, the punctuation symbols are (,) and ,. To avoid having formulas cluttered with brackets, we adopt the following precedence hierarchy, with the highest precedence at the top:

$$\sim, \forall, \exists$$
$$\vee$$
$$\wedge$$

Next we turn to the definition of the first order language given by an alphabet.

Definition A *term* is defined inductively as follows:
(a) A variable is a term.
(b) A constant is a term.
(c) If f is an n-ary function and $t_1,...,t_n$ are terms, then $f(t_1,...,t_n)$ is a term.

Definition A (*well-formed*) *formula* is defined inductively as follows:
(a) If p is an n-ary predicate and $t_1,...,t_n$ are terms, then $p(t_1,...,t_n)$ is a formula (called an *atomic formula* or, more simply, an *atom*).
(b) If F and G are formulas, then so are (~F), (F∧G), (F∨G), (F→G) and (F↔G).
(c) If F is a formula and x is a variable, then (∀x F) and (∃x F) are formulas.

It will often be convenient to write the formula (F→G) as (G←F).

Definition The *first order language* given by an alphabet consists of the set of all formulas constructed from the symbols of the alphabet.

Example (∀x (∃y (p(x,y)→q(x)))), (~(∃x (p(x,a)∧q(f(x))))) and (∀x (p(x,g(x))←(q(x)∧(~r(x))))) are formulas. By dropping pairs of brackets when no confusion is possible and using the above precedence convention, we can write these formulas more simply as ∀x∃y (p(x,y)→q(x)), ~∃x (p(x,a)∧q(f(x))) and ∀x (p(x,g(x))←q(x)∧~r(x)). We will simplify formulas in this way wherever possible.

The informal semantics of the quantifiers and connectives is as follows. ~ is negation, ∧ is conjunction (and), ∨ is disjunction (or), → is implication and ↔ is equivalence. Also, ∃ is the existential quantifier, so that "∃x" means "there exists an x", while ∀ is the universal quantifier, so that "∀x" means "for all x". Thus the informal semantics of ∀x (p(x,g(x))←q(x)∧~r(x)) is "for every x, if q(x) is true and r(x) is false, then p(x,g(x)) is true".

Definition The *scope* of ∀x (resp. ∃x) in ∀x F (resp. ∃x F) is F. A *bound occurrence* of a variable in a formula is an occurrence immediately following a quantifier or an occurrence within the scope of a quantifier, which has the same variable immediately after the quantifier. Any other occurrence of a variable is *free.*

Example In the formula ∃x p(x,y)∧q(x), the first two occurrences of x are bound, while the third occurrence is free, since the scope of ∃x is p(x,y). In ∃x (p(x,y)∧q(x)), all occurrences of x are bound, since the scope of ∃x is p(x,y)∧q(x).

Definition A *closed formula* is a formula with no free occurrences of any variable.

Example ∀y∃x (p(x,y)∧q(x)) is closed. However, ∃x (p(x,y)∧q(x)) is not closed, since there is a free occurrence of the variable y.

Definition If F is a formula, then ∀(F) denotes the *universal closure* of F, which is the closed formula obtained by adding a universal quantifier for every variable having a free occurrence in F. Similarly, ∃(F) denotes the *existential closure* of F, which is obtained by adding an existential quantifier for every variable having a free occurrence in F.

Example If F is p(x,y)∧q(x), then ∀(F) is ∀x∀y (p(x,y)∧q(x)), while ∃(F) is ∃x∃y (p(x,y)∧q(x)).

Next we introduce an important class of formulas called clauses.

Definition A *literal* is an atom or the negation of an atom. A *positive literal* is just an atom. A *negative literal* is the negation of an atom.

Definition A *clause* is a formula of the form

$$\forall x_1 \ldots \forall x_s \, (L_1 \vee \ldots \vee L_m)$$

where each L_i is a literal and $x_1, \ldots, x_s$ are all the variables occurring in $L_1 \vee \ldots \vee L_m$.

Example The following are clauses

$$\forall x \forall y \forall z \, (p(x,z) \vee \sim q(x,y) \vee \sim r(y,z))$$
$$\forall x \forall y \, (\sim p(x,y) \vee r(f(x,y),a))$$

Because clauses are so common in logic programming, it will be convenient to adopt a special clausal notation. Throughout, we will denote the clause

$$\forall x_1 \ldots \forall x_s \, (A_1 \vee \ldots \vee A_k \vee \sim B_1 \vee \ldots \vee \sim B_n)$$

in these atoms, by

$$A_1,\ldots,A_k \leftarrow B_1,\ldots,B_n$$

Thus, in the clausal notation, all variables are assumed to be universally quantified, the commas in the antecedent $B_1,\ldots,B_n$ denote conjunction and the commas in the consequent $A_1,\ldots,A_k$ denote disjunction. These conventions are justified because

$$\forall x_1\ldots\forall x_s\ (A_1 \vee\ldots\vee A_k \vee \sim B_1 \vee\ldots\vee \sim B_n)$$

is equivalent to

$$\forall x_1\ldots\forall x_s\ (A_1 \vee\ldots\vee A_k \leftarrow B_1 \wedge\ldots\wedge B_n)$$

Definition A *program clause* is a clause of the form

$$A \leftarrow B_1,\ldots,B_n$$

which contains precisely one positive literal (viz. A). A is called the *head* and $B_1,\ldots,B_n$ is called the *body* of the program clause.

Definition A *unit clause* is a clause of the form

$$A \leftarrow$$

that is, a program clause with an empty body.

The informal semantics of $A \leftarrow B_1,\ldots,B_n$ is "for each assignment of each variable, if $B_1,\ldots,B_n$ are all true, then A is true". Thus, if $n>0$, a program clause is conditional. On the other hand, a unit clause $A \leftarrow$ is unconditional. Its informal semantics is "for each assignment of each variable, A is true".

Now we are in a position to give the definition of a logic program.

Definition A *logic program* is a finite set of program clauses.

Definition In a logic program, the set of all program clauses with the same predicate p in the head is called the *definition* of p.

Example The following logic program, called slowsort, sorts a list of non-negative integers into a list in which the elements are in increasing order. It is a very inefficient sorting program! However, we will find it most useful for illustrating various aspects of the theory.

In this program, non-negative integers are represented using a constant 0 and a unary function f. The intended meaning of 0 is zero and f is the successor function. We define the powers of f by induction: $f^0(x)=0$ and $f^{n+1}(x)=f(f^n(x))$. Then the non-negative integer n is represented by the term

$f^n(0)$. In fact, it will sometimes be convenient to simply denote $f^n(0)$ by n.

Lists are represented using a binary function . (the cons function written infix) and the constant nil representing the empty list. Thus the list [17, 22, 6, 5] would be represented by 17.(22.(6.(5.nil))). We make the usual right associativity convention and write this more simply as 17.22.6.5.nil.

SLOWSORT PROGRAM

sort(x,y) ← sorted(y), perm(x,y)
sorted(nil) ←
sorted(x.nil) ←
sorted(x.y.z) ← x≤y, sorted(y.z)
perm(nil,nil) ←
perm(x.y,u.v) ← delete(u,x.y,z), perm(z,v)
delete(x,x.y,y) ←
delete(x,y.z,y.w) ← delete(x,z,w)
0≤x ←
f(x)≤f(y) ← x≤y

Slowsort contains definitions of five predicates, sort, sorted, perm, delete and ≤ (written infix). The informal semantics of the definition of sort is "if x and y are lists, y is a permutation of x and y is sorted, then y is the sorted version of x". This is clearly a correct top-level description of a sorting program. Similarly, the first clause in the definition of sorted states that "the empty list is sorted". The intended meaning of the predicate delete is that delete(x,y,z) should hold if z is the list obtained by deleting the element x from the list y. The above definition for delete contains obviously correct statements about the delete predicate.

Definition A *goal clause* is a clause of the form

$$\leftarrow B_1,\ldots,B_n$$

that is, a clause which has an empty consequent. Each B_i (i=1,...,n) is called a *subgoal* of the goal clause.

If $y_1,\ldots,y_r$ are the variables of the goal clause

$$\leftarrow B_1,\ldots,B_n$$

then this clausal notation is shorthand for

$$\forall y_1 \ldots \forall y_r \, (\sim B_1 \vee \ldots \vee \sim B_n)$$

or, equivalently,

$$\sim \exists y_1 \ldots \exists y_r \, (B_1 \wedge \ldots \wedge B_n)$$

Example To run slowsort, we give it a goal clause such as

$$\leftarrow \text{sort}(17.22.6.5.\text{nil},y)$$

This is understood as a request to find the list y, which is the sorted version of 17.22.6.5.nil.

Definition The *empty clause*, denoted □, is the clause with empty consequent and empty antecedent. This clause is to be understood as a contradiction.

Definition A *Horn clause* is a clause which is either a program clause or a goal clause.

We will find it convenient to abbreviate "logic program" to "program" and "goal clause" to "goal" throughout.

§3. MODELS OF LOGIC PROGRAMS

The declarative semantics of a program is given by the usual (model-theoretic) semantics of formulas in first order logic. This section discusses interpretations and models, concentrating particularly on the important class of Herbrand interpretations.

Before we give the main definitions, some motivation is appropriate. In order to be able to discuss the truth or falsity of formulas, it is first necessary to attach some meaning to each of the symbols in the formula. The various quantifiers and connectives have a fixed meaning, but the meaning attached to the constants, functions and predicates can vary. An interpretation simply consists of some domain of discourse over which the variables range, the assignment of each constant to an element of the domain, the assignment of each function to a mapping on the domain and the assignment of each predicate to a relation on the domain. Each interpretation thus specifies a meaning for each symbol in the formula. We are particularly interested in interpretations for which the formula expresses a true statement in that interpretation. Such an interpretation is called a model of the formula. Normally there is some distinguished interpretation, called the *intended* interpretation, which gives the principal meaning of the symbols. Naturally, the intended interpretation should be a model.

First order logic provides methods for deducing the theorems of a theory. These can be characterized (by Godel's completenesss theorem [42], [56]) as the formulas which are logical consequences of the axioms of the theory, that is, they are true in every interpretation which is a model of each of the axioms of the theory. In particular, each theorem is true in the intended interpretation of the theory. The logic programming systems in which we are interested use the resolution rule as the only inference rule. Suppose we want to prove that the formula

$$\exists y_1 \ldots \exists y_r\, (B_1 \wedge \ldots \wedge B_n)$$

is a logical consequence of a program P. Now resolution theorem provers are refutation systems. That is, the negation of the formula to be proved is added to the axioms and a contradiction is derived. If we negate the formula we want to prove, we obtain the goal

$$\leftarrow B_1, \ldots, B_n$$

Working top-down from this goal, the system derives successive goals. If the empty clause is eventually derived, then a contradiction has been obtained and later results assure us that

$$\exists y_1 \ldots \exists y_r\, (B_1 \wedge \ldots \wedge B_n)$$

is indeed a logical consequence of P.

From a theorem proving point of view, the only interest is to demonstrate logical consequence. However, from a programming point of view, we are much more interested in the bindings that have been made for the variables $y_1, \ldots, y_r$, because these give us the *output* from the running of the program. In fact, the ideal view of a logic programming system is that it is a black box for computing bindings and our only interest is in its input-output behaviour. The internal workings of the system should be invisible to the programmer. Unfortunately, this situation is not true, to various extents, with current PROLOG systems. Many programs can only be understood in a procedural (i.e. operational) manner, because of the way they use cuts and other non-logical features.

Returning to the slowsort program, from a theorem proving point of view, we can regard the goal ←sort(17.22.6.5.nil,y) as a request to prove that ∃y sort(17.22.6.5.nil,y) is a logical consequence of the program. In fact, we are much more interested that the proof is constructive and provides us with a specific y which makes sort(17.22.6.5.nil,y) true in the intended interpretation.

We now give the definitions of interpretations and models.

Definition An *interpretation* of a first order language L consists of the following:

(a) A non-empty set D, called the *domain* of the interpretation.

(b) For each constant in L, the assignment of an element in D.

(c) For each n-ary function in L, the assignment of a mapping from D^n to D.

(d) For each n-ary predicate in L, the assignment of a mapping from D^n into {true, false} (or, equivalently, a relation on D^n).

Definition Let I be an interpretation of a first order language L. A *variable assignment* (*wrt* I) is an assignment to each variable in L of an element in the domain of I.

Definition Let I be an interpretation with domain D of a first order language L and let A be a variable assignment. The *term assignment* (*wrt* I *and* A) of the terms in L is defined as follows:

(a) Each variable is given its assignment according to A.

(b) Each constant is given its assignment according to I.

(c) If $t_1',...,t_n'$ are the term assignments of $t_1,...,t_n$ and f' is the assignment of f, then $f'(t_1',...,t_n') \in D$ is the term assignment of $f(t_1,...,t_n)$.

Definition Let I be an interpretation with domain D of a first order language L and let A be a variable assignment. Then a formula in L can be given a *truth value*, true or false, (*wrt* I *and* A) as follows:

(a) If the formula is an atom $p(t_1,...,t_n)$, then the truth value is obtained by calculating the value of $p'(t_1',...,t_n')$, where p' is the mapping assigned to p by I and $t_1',...,t_n'$ are the term assignments of $t_1,...,t_n$ wrt I and A.

(b) If the formula has the form $\sim F$, $F \wedge G$, $F \vee G$, $F \rightarrow G$ or $F \longleftrightarrow G$, then the truth value of the formula is given by the following table:

F	G	$\sim F$	$F \wedge G$	$F \vee G$	$F \rightarrow G$	$F \longleftrightarrow G$
true	true	false	true	true	true	true
true	false	false	false	true	false	false
false	true	true	false	true	true	false
false	false	true	false	false	true	true

(c) If the formula has the form $\exists x\ F$, then the truth value of the formula is true if there exists $d \in D$ such that F has truth value true wrt I and A(x/d), where A(x/d) is A except that x is assigned d; otherwise, its truth value is false.

(d) If the formula has the form $\forall x\, F$, then the truth value of the formula is true if, for all $d \in D$, we have that F has truth value true wrt I and A(x/d); otherwise, its truth value is false.

Clearly the truth value of a closed formula does not depend on the variable assignment. Consequently, we can speak unambiguously of the truth value of a closed formula wrt to an interpretation.

Definition Let I be an interpretation of a first order language L and let F be a closed formula of L. Then I is a *model* for F if the truth value of F wrt I is true.

The axioms of a first order theory are a designated subset of closed formulas in the language of the theory. For example, the first order theories in which we are most interested have the clauses of a program as their axioms.

Definition Let T be a first order theory and let L be the language of T. A *model* for T is an interpretation for L which is a model for each axiom of T.

Example Consider the formula $\forall x \exists y\, p(x,y)$ and the following interpretation I. Let the domain D be the non-negative integers and let p be assigned the relation $<$. Then I is a model of the formula, as is easily seen. In I, the formula expresses the true statement that "for every non-negative integer, there exists a non-negative integer which is strictly larger than it". On the other hand, I is not a model of the formula $\exists y \forall x\, p(x,y)$.

The concept of a model of a closed formula can easily be extended to a set of closed formulas.

Definition Let S be a set of closed formulas of a first order language L and let I be an interpretation of L. We say I is a *model* for S if I is a model for each formula of S.

Note that if $S = \{F_1,...,F_n\}$ is a finite set of closed formulas, then I is a model for S iff I is a model for $F_1 \wedge ... \wedge F_n$.

We say S is *satisfiable* if L has an interpretation which is a model for S. S is *valid* if every interpretation of L is a model for S. S is *unsatisfiable* if it has no models.

Now we can give the definition of the important concept of logical consequence.

Definition Let S be a set of closed formulas and F be a closed formula of a first order language L. We say F is a *logical consequence* of S if, for every interpretation I of L, I is a model for S implies that I is a model for F.

Note that if $S = \{F_1,...,F_n\}$ is a finite set of closed formulas, then F is a logical consequence of S iff $F_1 \wedge ... \wedge F_n \rightarrow F$ is valid.

Proposition 3.1 Let S be a set of closed formulas and F be a closed formula of a first order language L. Then F is a logical consequence of S iff $S \cup \{\sim F\}$ is unsatisfiable.

Proof Suppose that F is a logical consequence of S. Let I be an interpretation of L and suppose I is a model for S. Then I is also a model for F. Hence I is not a model for $S \cup \{\sim F\}$. Thus $S \cup \{\sim F\}$ is unsatisfiable.

Conversely, suppose $S \cup \{\sim F\}$ is unsatisfiable. Let I be any interpretation of L. Suppose I is a model for S. Since $S \cup \{\sim F\}$ is unsatisfiable, I cannot be a model for ~F. Thus I is a model for F and so F is a logical consequence of S ∎

Example Let $S = \{p(a), \forall x\,(p(x) \rightarrow q(x))\}$ and F be q(a). We show that F is a logical consequence of S. Let I be any model for S. Thus p(a) is true wrt I. It follows from this and the truth of $\forall x\,(p(x) \rightarrow q(x))$ that q(a) must be true wrt I.

Applying these definitions to programs, we see that when we give a goal G to the system, with program P loaded, we are asking the system to show that the set of clauses $P \cup \{G\}$ is unsatisfiable. In fact, if G is the goal $\leftarrow B_1,...,B_n$ with variables $y_1,...,y_r$, then proposition 3.1 states that showing $P \cup \{G\}$ unsatisfiable is exactly the same as showing that $\exists y_1 ... \exists y_r\,(B_1 \wedge ... \wedge B_n)$ is a logical consequence of P.

Thus the basic problem is that of determining the unsatisfiability, or otherwise, of $P \cup \{G\}$, where P is a program and G is a goal. According to the definition, this implies showing *every* interpretation of $P \cup \{G\}$ is not a model. Needless to say, this seems to be a formidable problem. However, it turns out that there is a much smaller and more convenient class of interpretations, which are all that need to be investigated to show unsatisfiability. These are the so-called Herbrand interpretations, which we now proceed to study.

Definition A *ground term* is a term not containing variables. Similarly, a *ground atom* is an atom not containing variables.

Definition Let L be a first order language. The *Herbrand universe* U_L for L is the set of all ground terms, which can be formed out of the constants and functions appearing in L. (In the case that L has no constants, we add some constant, say, a, to form ground terms).

Example Consider the program

$p(x) \leftarrow q(f(x),g(x))$

$r(y) \leftarrow$

which has an underlying first order language L based on the predicates p, q and r and the functions f and g. Then the Herbrand universe for L is

$$\{a, f(a), g(a), f(f(a)), f(g(a)), g(f(a)), g(g(a)), \ldots\}.$$

Definition Let L be a first order language. The *Herbrand base* B_L for L is the set of all ground atoms which can be formed by using predicates from L with ground terms from the Herbrand universe as arguments.

Example For the previous example, the Herbrand base for L is

$$\{p(a), q(a,a), r(a), p(f(a)), p(g(a)), q(a,f(a)), q(f(a),a), \ldots\}.$$

Definition Let L be a first order language. An interpretation for L is a *Herbrand interpretation* if the following conditions are satisfied:

(a) The domain of the interpretation is the Herbrand universe U_L.

(b) Constants in L are assigned to "themselves" in U_L.

(c) If f is an n-ary function in L, then f is assigned to the mapping from $(U_L)^n$ into U_L defined by $(t_1,\ldots,t_n) \rightarrow f(t_1,\ldots,t_n)$.

We make no restriction on the assignment of the predicates in L, so that different Herbrand interpretations arise by taking different such assignments. Since, for Herbrand interpretations, the assignment of constants and functions the Herbrand base. For any Herbrand interpretation, the corresponding subset of the Herbrand base is the set of all ground atoms which are true wrt the interpretation. Conversely, given an arbitrary subset of the Herbrand base, there is a corresponding Herbrand interpretation defined by specifying that predicates map to "true" precisely when the predicate applied to its arguments is in the given subset. This identification of a Herbrand interpretation as a subset of the Herbrand base will be made throughout.

Definition Let L be a first order language and S a set of closed formulas of L. A *Herbrand model* for S is a Herbrand interpretation for L which is a model for S.

It will often be convenient to refer, by abuse of language, to an interpretation of a set S of formulas rather than the underlying first order language from which the formulas come. Normally, we assume that the underlying first order language is defined by the constants, functions and predicates appearing in S. With this understanding, we can now refer to the Herbrand universe U_S and Herbrand base B_S of S and also refer to Herbrand interpretations of S as subsets of the Herbrand base of S. In particular, the set of formulas will often be a program P, so that we will refer to the Herbrand universe U_P and Herbrand base B_P of P.

Example We now illustrate these concepts with the slowsort program. This program can be regarded as the set of axioms of a first order theory. The language of this theory is given by the constants 0 and nil, functions f and . and predicates sort, perm, sorted, delete and $\leq$. The only inference rule is the resolution rule. The intended interpretation is a Herbrand interpretation. An atom sort(l,m) is in the intended interpretation iff each of l and m is either nil or is a list of terms of the form $f^k(0)$ and m is the sorted version of l. The other predicates have the obvious assignments. The intended interpretation is indeed a model for the program and hence a model for the associated theory.

Next we show that in order to prove unsatisfiability of a set of clauses, it suffices to consider only Herbrand interpretations.

Proposition 3.2 Let S be a set of clauses and suppose S has a model. Then S has a Herbrand model.

Proof Let I be an interpretation of S. We define a Herbrand interpretation I′ of S as follows:

$$I' = \{p(t_1,\ldots,t_n) \in B_S : p(t_1,\ldots,t_n) \text{ is true wrt } I\}.$$

It is straightforward to show that if I is a model, then I′ is also a model ∎

Proposition 3.3 Let S be a set of clauses. Then S is unsatisfiable iff S has no Herbrand models.

Proof If S is satisfiable, then proposition 3.2 shows that it has a Herbrand model ∎

It is important to understand that neither proposition 3.2 nor 3.3 holds if we drop the restriction that S be a set of *clauses*. In other words, if S is a set of *arbitrary* closed formulas, it is not generally possible to show S is unsatisfiable by restricting attention to Herbrand interpretations.

Example Let S be {p(a), ∃x ~p(x)}. Note that the second formula in S is not a clause. We claim that S has a model. It suffices to let D be the set {0, 1}, assign a to 0 and assign p to the mapping which maps 0 to true and 1 to false. Clearly this gives a model for S.

However, S does not have a Herbrand model. The only Herbrand interpretations for S are ∅ (the empty set) and {p(a)}. But neither of these is a model for S.

The point is worth emphasizing. Much of the theory of logic programming is concerned only with clauses and for this Herbrand interpretations suffice. However, non-clausal formulas do arise naturally (particularly in chapter 3). For this part of the theory, we will be forced to consider arbitrary interpretations.

§4. ANSWER SUBSTITUTIONS

Earlier we stated that the main purpose of a logic programming system is to compute bindings. In this section, we introduce the important concept of a correct answer substitution, which provides a declarative understanding of the desired output from a program and a goal. We also present a detailed discussion of unifiers and the unification algorithm.

Definition A *substitution* θ is a finite set of the form $\{v_1/t_1,...,v_n/t_n\}$, where each v_i is a variable, each t_i is a term distinct from v_i and the variables $v_1,...,v_n$ are distinct. Each element v_i/t_i is called a *binding* for v_i. θ is called a *ground substitution* if the t_i are all ground terms. θ is called a *variable-pure substitution* if the t_i are all variables.

Definition An *expression* is either a term, a literal or a conjunction or disjunction of literals. A *simple expression* is either a term or an atom.

Definition Let $\theta = \{v_1/t_1,...,v_n/t_n\}$ be a substitution and E be an expression. Then $E\theta$, the *instance* of E by θ, is the expression obtained from E by simultaneously replacing each occurrence of the variable v_i in E by the term t_i (i=1,...,n). If $E\theta$ is ground, then $E\theta$ is called a *ground instance* of E.

Example Let E = p(x,y,f(a)) and $\theta = \{x/b, y/x\}$. Then $E\theta$ = p(b,x,f(a)).

If $S = \{E_1,...,E_n\}$ is a finite set of expressions and θ is a substitution, then $S\theta$ denotes the set $\{E_1\theta,...,E_n\theta\}$.

Definition Let $\theta = \{u_1/s_1,...,u_m/s_m\}$ and $\sigma = \{v_1/t_1,...,v_n/t_n\}$ be substitutions. Then the *composition* $\theta\sigma$ of θ and σ is the substitution obtained from the set

$$\{u_1/s_1\sigma,...,u_m/s_m\sigma,\ v_1/t_1,...,v_n/t_n\}$$

by deleting any binding $u_i/s_i\sigma$ for which $u_i=s_i\sigma$ and deleting any binding v_j/t_j for which $v_j \in \{u_1,...,u_m\}$.

Example Let $\theta = \{x/f(y), y/z\}$ and $\sigma = \{x/a, y/b, z/y\}$. Then $\theta\sigma = \{x/f(b), z/y\}$.

Definition The substitution given by the empty set is called the *identity substitution.*

We denote the identity substitution by ϵ. Note that $E\epsilon = E$, for all expressions E. The elementary properties of substitutions are contained in the following proposition.

Proposition 4.1 Let θ, σ and γ be substitutions. Then
(a) $\theta\epsilon = \epsilon\theta = \theta$.
(b) $(E\theta)\sigma = E(\theta\sigma)$, for all expressions E.
(c) $(\theta\sigma)\gamma = \theta(\sigma\gamma)$.

Proof (a) This follows immediately from the definition of ϵ.

(b) Clearly it suffices to prove the result when E is a variable, say, x. Let $\theta = \{u_1/s_1,\ldots,u_m/s_m\}$ and $\sigma = \{v_1/t_1,\ldots,v_n/t_n\}$. If $x \notin \{u_1,\ldots,u_m\} \cup \{v_1,\ldots,v_n\}$, then $(x\theta)\sigma = x = x(\theta\sigma)$. If $x \in \{u_1,\ldots,u_m\}$, say $x=u_i$, then $(x\theta)\sigma = s_i\sigma = x(\theta\sigma)$. If $x \in \{v_1,\ldots,v_n\} \backslash \{u_1,\ldots,u_m\}$, say $x=v_j$, then $(x\theta)\sigma = t_j = x(\theta\sigma)$.

(c) Clearly it suffices to show that if x is a variable, then $x((\theta\sigma)\gamma) = x(\theta(\sigma\gamma))$. In fact, $x((\theta\sigma)\gamma) = (x(\theta\sigma))\gamma = ((x\theta)\sigma)\gamma = (x\theta)(\sigma\gamma) = x(\theta(\sigma\gamma))$, by (b) ▮

Proposition 4.1(a) shows that ϵ acts as a left and right identity for composition. The definition of composition of substitutions was made precisely in order to be able obtain (b). Note that (c) shows that we can omit parentheses when writing a composition $\theta_1\ldots\theta_n$ of substitutions.

Example Let $\theta = \{x/f(y), y/z\}$ and $\sigma = \{x/a, z/b\}$. Then $\theta\sigma = \{x/f(y), y/b, z/b\}$. Let $E = p(x,y,g(z))$. Then $E\theta = p(f(y),z,g(z))$ and $(E\theta)\sigma = p(f(y),b,g(b))$. Also $E(\theta\sigma) = p(f(y),b,g(b)) = (E\theta)\sigma$.

Definition Let E and F be expressions. We say E and F are ***variants*** if there exist substitutions θ and σ such that $E=F\theta$ and $F=E\sigma$. We also say E is a variant of F or F is a variant of E.

Example p(f(x,y),g(z),a) is a variant of p(f(y,x),g(u),a). However, p(x,x) is not a variant of p(x,y).

Definition Let E be an expression and V be the set of variables occurring in E. A ***renaming substitution*** for E is a variable-pure substitution $\{x_1/y_1,\ldots,x_n/y_n\}$ such that $\{x_1,\ldots,x_n\} \subseteq V$, the y_i are distinct and $(V\backslash\{x_1,\ldots,x_n\}) \cap \{y_1,\ldots,y_n\} = \emptyset$.

Proposition 4.2 Let E and F be expressions which are variants. Then there exist substitutions θ and σ such that $E=F\theta$ and $F=E\sigma$, where θ is a renaming substitution for F and σ is a renaming substitution for E.

Proof Since E and F are variants, there exist substitutions θ_1 and σ_1 such that $E=F\theta_1$ and $F=E\sigma_1$. Let V be the set of variables occurring in E and let σ be the substitution obtained from σ_1 by deleting all bindings of the follows that σ must be a renaming substitution for E ∎

We will be particularly interested in substitutions which unify a set of expressions, that is, make each expression in the set syntactically identical. The concept of unification goes back to Herbrand [27] in 1930. It was rediscovered in 1960 by Prawitz [50] and further exploited by Robinson [51] for use in the resolution rule. We restrict attention to (non-empty) finite sets of simple expressions, which is all that we require. Recall that a simple expression is a term or an atom.

Definition Let S be a finite set of simple expressions. A substitution θ is called a *unifier* for S if $S\theta$ is a singleton. A unifier θ for S is called a *most general unifier* (mgu) for S, if for each unifier σ of S, there exists a substitution γ such that $\sigma=\theta\gamma$.

Example {p(f(x),a), p(y,f(w))} is not unifiable, because the second arguments cannot be unified.

Example {p(f(x),z), p(y,a)} is unifiable, since σ = {y/f(a), x/a, z/a} is a unifier. A most general unifier is θ = {y/f(x), z/a}. Note that $\sigma = \theta$ {x/a}.

It follows from the definition of an mgu that if θ and σ are both mgu's of $\{E_1,...,E_n\}$, then $E_1\theta$ is a variant of $E_1\sigma$. Proposition 4.2 then shows that $E_1\sigma$ can be obtained from $E_1\theta$ simply by renaming variables. Thus mgu's are unique modulo renaming.

We next present an algorithm, called the unification algorithm, which takes a finite set of simple expressions as input and outputs an mgu if the set is unifiable. Otherwise, it reports the fact that the set is not unifiable. The intuitive idea behind the unification algorithm is as follows. Suppose we want to unify two simple expressions. Imagine two pointers, one at the leftmost symbol of each of the two expressions. The pointers are moved together to the right until they point to different symbols. An attempt is made to unify the two subexpressions starting with these symbols by making a substitution. If the attempt is successful, the process is continued with the two expressions obtained by applying the substitution. If not, the expressions are not unifiable. If the pointers eventually reach the end of the two expressions, the composition of all the substitutions made is an mgu of the two expressions.

Definition Let S be a finite set of simple expressions. The *disagreement set* of S is defined as follows. Locate the leftmost symbol position at which not all expressions in S have the same symbol and extract from each expression in S the subexpression beginning at that symbol position. The set of all such subexpressions is the disagreement set.

Example Let S = {p(f(x),h(y),a), p(f(x),z,a), p(f(x),h(y),b)}. Then the disagreement set is {h(y), z}.

We now present the unification algorithm. In this algorithm, S denotes a finite set of simple expressions.

UNIFICATION ALGORITHM

1. Put k=0 and $\sigma_0 = \epsilon$.
2. If $S\sigma_k$ is a singleton, then stop; σ_k is an mgu of S. Otherwise, find the disagreement set D_k of $S\sigma_k$.
3. If there exist v and t in D_k such that v is a variable that does not occur in t, then put $\sigma_{k+1} = \sigma_k\{v/t\}$, increment k and go to 2. Otherwise, stop; S is not unifiable.

The unification algorithm as presented above is non-deterministic to the extent that there may be several choices for v and t in step 3. However, as we remarked earlier, the application of any two mgu's produced by the algorithm leads to expressions which differ only by a change of variable names. It is clear that the algorithm terminates because S contains only finitely many variables and each application of step 3 eliminates one variable.

Example Let S = {p(f(a),g(x)), p(y,y)}.

(a) $\sigma_0 = \epsilon$.
(b) D_0 = {f(a), y}, σ_1 = {y/f(a)} and $S\sigma_1$ = {p(f(a),g(x)), p(f(a),f(a))}.
(c) D_1 = {g(x), f(a)}. Thus S is not unifiable.

Example Let S = {p(a,x,h(g(z))), p(z,h(y),h(y))}.

(a) $\sigma_0 = \epsilon$.
(b) D_0 = {a, z}, σ_1 = {z/a} and $S\sigma_1$ = {p(a,x,h(g(a))), p(a,h(y),h(y))}.
(c) D_1 = {x, h(y)}, σ_2 = {z/a, x/h(y)} and $S\sigma_2$ = {p(a,h(y),h(g(a))), p(a,h(y),h(y))}.
(d) D_2 = {y, g(a)}, σ_3 = {z/a, x/h(g(a)), y/g(a)} and $S\sigma_3$ =

In step 3 of the unification algorithm, a check is made to see whether v occurs in t. This is called the *occur check.* The next example illustrates the use of the occur check.

Example Let S = {p(x,x), p(y,f(y))}.

(a) $\sigma_0 = \epsilon$.

(b) D_0 = {x, y}, σ_1 = {x/y} and $S\sigma_1$ = {p(y,y), p(y,f(y))}.

(c) D_1 = {y, f(y)}. Since y occurs in f(y), S is not unifiable.

Next we prove that the unification algorithm does indeed find an mgu of a unifiable set of simple expressions. This result first appeared in [51].

Theorem 4.3 (Unification theorem)

Let S be a finite set of simple expressions. If S is unifiable, then the unification algorithm terminates and gives an mgu for S. If S is not unifiable, then the unification algorithm terminates and reports this fact.

Proof We have already noted that the unification algorithm always terminates. It suffices to show that if S is unifiable, then the algorithm finds an mgu. In fact, if S is not unifiable, then the algorithm cannot terminate at step 2 and, since it does terminate, it must terminate at step 3. Thus it does report the fact that S is not unifiable.

Assume then that S is unifiable and let θ be any unifier for S. We prove first that, for $k \geq 0$, if σ_k is the substitution given in the kth iteration of the algorithm, then there exists a substitution γ_k such that $\theta = \sigma_k\gamma_k$.

Suppose first that k=0. Then we can put $\gamma_0 = \theta$, since $\theta = \epsilon\theta$. Next suppose, for some $k>0$, there exists γ_k such that $\theta = \sigma_k\gamma_k$. If $S\sigma_k$ is a singleton, then the algorithm terminates at step 2. Hence we can confine attention to the case when $S\sigma_k$ is not a singleton. We want to show that the algorithm will produce a further substitution σ_{k+1} and that there exists a substitution γ_{k+1} such that $\theta = \sigma_{k+1}\gamma_{k+1}$.

Since $S\sigma_k$ is not a singleton, the algorithm will determine the disagreement set D_k of $S\sigma_k$ and go to step 3. Since $\theta = \sigma_k\gamma_k$ and θ unifies S, it follows that γ_k unifies D_k. Thus D_k must contain a variable, say, v. Let t be any other term in D_k. Then v cannot occur in t because $v\gamma_k = t\gamma_k$. We can suppose that {v/t} is indeed the substitution chosen at step 3. Thus $\sigma_{k+1} = \sigma_k\{v/t\}$.

We now define $\gamma_{k+1} = \gamma_k \setminus \{v/v\gamma_k\}$. If γ_k has a binding for v, then

$$\begin{aligned}\gamma_k &= \{v/v\gamma_k\} \cup \gamma_{k+1}\\ &= \{v/t\gamma_k\} \cup \gamma_{k+1}\\ &= \{v/t\gamma_{k+1}\} \cup \gamma_{k+1} && \text{(since v does not occur in t)}\\ &= \{v/t\}\gamma_{k+1} && \text{(by the definition of composition).}\end{aligned}$$

If γ_k does not have a binding for v, then $\gamma_{k+1} = \gamma_k$, each element of D_k is a variable and $\gamma_k = \{v/t\}\gamma_{k+1}$. Thus $\theta = \sigma_k\gamma_k = \sigma_k\{v/t\}\gamma_{k+1} = \sigma_{k+1}\gamma_{k+1}$, as required.

Now we can complete the proof. If S is unifiable, then we have shown that the algorithm must terminate at step 2 and, if it terminates at the kth iteration, then $\theta = \sigma_k\gamma_k$, for some γ_k. Since σ_k is a unifier of S, this equality shows that it is indeed an mgu for S ∎

The unification algorithm which we have presented can be very inefficient. In the worst case, its running time can be an exponential function of the length of the input. Consider the following example, which is taken from [5]. Let $S = \{p(x_1,...,x_n),\ p(f(x_0,x_0),...,f(x_{n-1},x_{n-1}))\}$. Then $\sigma_1 = \{x_1/f(x_0,x_0)\}$ and $S\sigma_1 = \{p(f(x_0,x_0),x_2,...,x_n),\ p(f(x_0,x_0),f(f(x_0,x_0),f(x_0,x_0)),f(x_2,x_2),..., f(x_{n-1},x_{n-1}))\}$. The next substitution is $\sigma_2 = \{x_1/f(x_0,x_0),\ x_2/f(f(x_0,x_0), f(x_0,x_0))\}$, and so on. Note that the second atom in $S\sigma_n$ has 2^k-1 occurrences of f in its kth argument ($1 \leq k \leq n$). In particular, its last argument has 2^n-1 occurrences of f. Now recall that step 3 of the unification algorithm has the occur check. The performance of this check just for the last substitution will thus require exponential time.

Much more efficient unification algorithms are known. For example, [40] and [48] give linear algorithms (see also [41]). However, most PROLOG implementations have a different solution to the efficiency problem. Since the occur check is the main cause of the problem, it is simply omitted! From a theoretical viewpoint, this is a disaster because it destroys the soundness of SLD-resolution. We discuss this matter further in §7.

With the background material on substitutions completed, let us now turn to the definition of a correct answer substitution. This is a central concept in logic programming and provides much of the focus for the theoretical developments.

Definition Let P be a program and G be a goal. An *answer substitution*

It is understood that the substitution does not necessarily contain a binding for every variable in G. In particular, if G has no variables the only possible answer substitution is the identity substitution.

Definition Let P be a program, G be a goal $\leftarrow A_1,\ldots,A_k$ and θ be an answer substitution for $P \cup \{G\}$. We say that θ is a *correct answer substitution* for $P \cup \{G\}$ if $\forall((A_1 \wedge \ldots \wedge A_k)\theta)$ is a logical consequence of P.

Using proposition 3.1, we see that θ is a correct answer substitution iff $P \cup \{\sim\forall((A_1 \wedge \ldots \wedge A_k)\theta)\}$ is unsatisfiable. This definition of correct answer substitution captures the intuitive meaning of a "correct answer". It provides a declarative understanding of the desired output from a program and goal. Much of chapter 2 will be concerned with showing the equivalence between this declarative concept and the corresponding procedural one, which is defined by the refutation procedure used by the system.

As well as returning answer substitutions, a logic programming system can also return the answer "no". We say the answer "no" is *correct* if $P \cup \{G\}$ is satisfiable.

§5. FIXPOINTS

Associated with every program is a monotonic mapping which plays a very important role in the theory. This section introduces the requisite concepts and results concerning monotonic mappings and their fixpoints.

Definition Let S be a set. A *relation* R on S is a subset of $S \times S$.

We denote the fact that $(x,y) \in R$ by xRy.

Definition A relation R on a set S is a *partial order* if the following conditions are satisfied:

(a) xRx, for all $x \in S$.
(b) xRy and yRx imply $x=y$, for all $x,y \in S$.
(c) xRy and yRz imply xRz, for all $x,y,z \in S$.

Example Let S be a set and 2^S be the set of all subsets of S. Then set inclusion, $\subseteq$, is easily seen to be a partial order on 2^S.

We adopt the standard notation and use $\leq$ to denote a partial order. Thus we have (a) $x \leq x$, (b) $x \leq y$ and $y \leq x$ imply $x=y$ and (c) $x \leq y$ and $y \leq z$ imply $x \leq z$, for all $x,y,z \in S$.

Definition Let S be a set with partial order $\leq$. Then $a \in S$ is an *upper bound* of a subset X of S if $x \leq a$, for all $x \in X$. Similarly, $b \in S$ is a *lower bound* of X if $b \leq x$, for all $x \in X$.

Definition Let S be a set with a partial order $\leq$. Then $a \in S$ is the *least upper bound* of a subset X of S if a is an upper bound of X and, for all upper bounds a' of X, we have $a \leq a'$. Similarly, $b \in S$ is the *greatest lower bound* of a subset X of S if b is a lower bound of X and, for all lower bounds b' of X, we have $b' \leq b$.

The least upper bound of X is unique, if it exists, and is denoted by lub(X). Similarly, the greatest lower bound of X is unique, if it exists, and is denoted by glb(X).

Definition A partially ordered set L is a *complete lattice* if lub(X) and glb(X) exist, for every subset X of L.

We let $\top$ denote the *top element* lub(L) and $\bot$ denote the *bottom element* glb(L) of the complete lattice L.

Example In the previous example, 2^S under $\subseteq$ is a complete lattice. In fact, the least upper bound of a collection of subsets of S is their union and the greatest lower bound is their intersection. The top element is S and the bottom element is $\emptyset$.

Definition Let L be a complete lattice and $T : L \rightarrow L$ be a mapping. We say T is *monotonic* if $T(x) \leq T(y)$, whenever $x \leq y$.

Definition Let L be a complete lattice and $X \subseteq L$. We say X is *directed* if every finite subset of X has an upper bound in X.

Definition Let L be a complete lattice and $T : L \rightarrow L$ be a mapping. We say T is *continuous* if $T(\text{lub}(X)) = \text{lub}(T(X))$, for every directed subset X of L.

By taking $X = \{x,y\}$, we see that every continuous mapping is

Our interest in these definitions arises from the fact that for a program P, the collection of all Herbrand interpretations forms a complete lattice in a natural way and also because there is a continuous mapping associated with P defined on this lattice. Next we study fixpoints of mappings defined on lattices.

Definition Let L be a complete lattice and $T : L \rightarrow L$ be a mapping. We say $a \in L$ is the *least fixpoint* of T if a is a fixpoint (that is, $T(a)=a$) and for all fixpoints b of T, we have $a \leq b$. Similarly, we define *greatest fixpoint.*

The next result is a weak form of a theorem due to Tarski [57], which generalizes an earlier result due to Knaster and Tarski. For an interesting account of the history of propositions 5.1, 5.3 and 5.4, see [36].

Proposition 5.1 Let L be a complete lattice and $T : L \rightarrow L$ be monotonic. Then T has a least fixpoint, lfp(T), and a greatest fixpoint, gfp(T). Furthermore, $\text{lfp}(T) = \text{glb}\{x : T(x)=x\} = \text{glb}\{x : T(x) \leq x\}$ and $\text{gfp}(T) = \text{lub}\{x : T(x)=x\} = \text{lub}\{x : x \leq T(x)\}$.

Proof Put $G = \{x : T(x) \leq x\}$ and $g = \text{glb}(G)$. We show that $g \in G$. Now $g \leq x$, for all $x \in G$, so that by the monotonicity of T, we have $T(g) \leq T(x)$, for all $x \in G$. Thus $T(g) \leq x$, for all $x \in G$, and so $T(g) \leq g$, by the definition of glb. Hence $g \in G$.

Next we show that g is a fixpoint of T. It remains to show that $g \leq T(g)$. Now $T(g) \leq g$ implies $T(T(g)) \leq T(g)$ implies $T(g) \in G$. Hence $g \leq T(g)$, so that g is a fixpoint of T.

Now put $g' = \text{glb}\{x : T(x)=x\}$. Since g is a fixpoint, we have $g' \leq g$. On the other hand, $\{x : T(x)=x\} \subseteq \{x : T(x) \leq x\}$ and so $g \leq g'$. Thus we have $g=g'$ and the proof is complete for lfp(T).

The proof for gfp(T) is similar ∎

Proposition 5.2 Let L be a complete lattice and $T : L \rightarrow L$ be monotonic. Suppose $a \in L$ and $a \leq T(a)$. Then there exists a fixpoint a' of T such that $a \leq a'$. Similarly, if $b \in L$ and $T(b) \leq b$, then there exists a fixpoint b' of T such that $b' \leq b$.

Proof By proposition 5.1, it suffices to put $a'=\text{gfp}(T)$ and $b'=\text{lfp}(T)$ ∎

We will also require the concept of ordinal powers of T. First we recall some elementary properties of ordinal numbers, which we will refer to more simply as ordinals. Intuitively, the ordinals are what we use to count with. The first ordinal 0 is defined to be $\emptyset$. Then we define $1 = \{\emptyset\} = \{0\}$, $2 = \{\emptyset, \{\emptyset\}\} = \{0, 1\}$, $3 = \{\emptyset, \{\emptyset\}, \{\emptyset, \{\emptyset\}\}\} = \{0, 1, 2\}$, and so on. These are the finite ordinals, the non-negative integers. The first infinite ordinal is $\omega = \{0, 1, 2,...\}$, the set of all non-negative integers. We adopt the convention of denoting finite ordinals by roman letters n, m,..., while arbitrary ordinals will be denoted by greek letters α, β,.... We can specify an ordering $<$ on the collection of all ordinals by defining $\alpha<\beta$ if $\alpha\in\beta$. For example, $n<\omega$, for all finite ordinals n. We will normally write $n\in\omega$ rather than $n<\omega$. If α is an ordinal, the *successor* of α is the ordinal $\alpha+1 = \alpha \cup \{\alpha\}$, which is the least ordinal greater than α. $\alpha+1$ is then said to be a *successor ordinal.* For example, $1 = 0+1$, $2 = 1+1$, $3 = 2+1$, and so on. If α is a successor ordinal, say $\alpha = \beta+1$, we denote β by $\alpha-1$. An ordinal α is said to be a *limit ordinal* if it is not the successor of any ordinal. The smallest limit ordinal (apart from 0) is ω. After ω comes $\omega+1 = \omega \cup \{\omega\}$, $\omega+2 = (\omega+1)+1$, $\omega+3$, and so on. The next limit ordinal is $\omega2$, which is the set consisting of all n, where $n\in\omega$, and all $\omega+n$, where $n\in\omega$. Then comes $\omega2+1, \omega2+2,...,\omega3, \omega3+1,...,\omega4,...,\omega n,....$

We will also require the *principle of transfinite induction,* which is as follows. Let $P(\alpha)$ be a property of ordinals. Assume that for all ordinals β, if $P(\gamma)$ holds for all $\gamma<\beta$, then $P(\beta)$ holds. Then $P(\alpha)$ holds for all ordinals α.

Now we can give the definition of the ordinal powers of T.

Definition Let L be a complete lattice and $T : L\rightarrow L$ be monotonic. Then we define

$T\uparrow 0 = \bot$
$T\uparrow\alpha = T(T\uparrow(\alpha-1))$, if α is a successor ordinal
$T\uparrow\alpha = lub\{T\uparrow\beta : \beta<\alpha\}$, if α is a limit ordinal
$T\downarrow 0 = \top$
$T\downarrow\alpha = T(T\downarrow(\alpha-1))$, if α is a successor ordinal
$T\downarrow\alpha = glb\{T\downarrow\beta : \beta<\alpha\}$, if α is a limit ordinal

Next we give a well-known characterization of lfp(T) and gfp(T) in terms of ordinal powers of T.

Proposition 5.3 Let L be a complete lattice and $T : L\rightarrow L$ be monotonic.

there exist ordinals β_1 and β_2 such that $\gamma_1 \geq \beta_1$ implies $T\uparrow\gamma_1 = \text{lfp}(T)$ and $\gamma_2 \geq \beta_2$ implies $T\downarrow\gamma_2 = \text{gfp}(T)$.

Proof The proof for lfp(T) follows from (a) and (e) below. The proofs of (a), (b) and (c) use transfinite induction.

(a) For all α, $T\uparrow\alpha \leq \text{lfp}(T)$:

If α is a limit ordinal, then $T\uparrow\alpha = \text{lub}\{T\uparrow\beta : \beta<\alpha\} \leq \text{lfp}(T)$, by the induction hypothesis. If α is a successor ordinal, then $T\uparrow\alpha = T(T\uparrow(\alpha-1)) \leq T(\text{lfp}(T)) = \text{lfp}(T)$, by the induction hypothesis, the monotonicity of T and the fixpoint property.

(b) For all α, $T\uparrow\alpha \leq T\uparrow(\alpha+1)$:

If α is a successor ordinal, then $T\uparrow\alpha = T(T\uparrow(\alpha-1)) \leq T(T\uparrow\alpha) = T\uparrow(\alpha+1)$, using the induction hypothesis and monotonicity of T. If α is a limit ordinal, then $T\uparrow\alpha = \text{lub}\{T\uparrow\beta : \beta<\alpha\} \leq \text{lub}\{T\uparrow(\beta+1) : \beta<\alpha\} \leq T(\text{lub}\{T\uparrow\beta : \beta<\alpha\}) = T\uparrow(\alpha+1)$, using the induction hypothesis and monotonicity of T.

(c) For all α,β, $\alpha<\beta$ implies $T\uparrow\alpha \leq T\uparrow\beta$:

If β is a limit ordinal, then $T\uparrow\alpha \leq \text{lub}\{T\uparrow\gamma : \gamma<\beta\} = T\uparrow\beta$. If β is a successor ordinal, then $\alpha \leq \beta-1$ and so $T\uparrow\alpha \leq T\uparrow(\beta-1) \leq T\uparrow\beta$, using the induction hypothesis and (b).

(d) For all α,β, $\alpha<\beta$ and $T\uparrow\alpha = T\uparrow\beta$ imply $T\uparrow\alpha = \text{lfp}(T)$:

Now $T\uparrow\alpha \leq T\uparrow(\alpha+1) \leq T\uparrow\beta$, by (c). Hence $T\uparrow\alpha = T\uparrow(\alpha+1) = T(T\uparrow\alpha)$ and so $T\uparrow\alpha$ is a fixpoint. Furthermore, $T\uparrow\alpha = \text{lfp}(T)$, by (a).

(e) There exists β such that $\gamma \geq \beta$ implies $T\uparrow\gamma = \text{lfp}(T)$:

Let α be the least ordinal of cardinality greater than the cardinality of L. Suppose that $T\uparrow\delta \neq \text{lfp}(T)$, for all $\delta<\alpha$. Define $h:\alpha\rightarrow L$ by $h(\delta) = T\uparrow\delta$. Then, by (d), h is injective, which contradicts the choice of α. Thus $T\uparrow\beta = \text{lfp}(T)$, for some $\beta<\alpha$, and the result follows from (a) and (c).

The proof for gfp(T) is similar ∎

The least α such that $T\uparrow\alpha = \text{lfp}(T)$ is called the *closure ordinal* of T. The next result, which is usually attributed to Kleene, shows that under the stronger assumption that T is continuous, the closure ordinal of T is $\leq \omega$.

Proposition 5.4 Let L be a complete lattice and $T : L \rightarrow L$ be continuous. Then $\text{lfp}(T) = T\uparrow\omega$.

Proof By proposition 5.3, it suffices to show that $T\uparrow\omega$ is a fixpoint. Note that $\{T\uparrow n : n\in\omega\}$ is directed, since T is monotonic. But then $T(T\uparrow\omega) = T(\mathrm{lub}\{T\uparrow n : n\in\omega\}) = \mathrm{lub}\{T(T\uparrow n) : n\in\omega\} = T\uparrow\omega$, using the continuity of T ∎

The analogue of proposition 5.4 for gfp(T) does not hold, that is, gfp(T) may not be equal to $T\downarrow\omega$. A counterexample is given in the next section.

§6. LEAST HERBRAND MODEL

This section introduces the least Herbrand model of a program. This particular model plays a central role in the theory. We show that the least Herbrand model is precisely the set of ground atoms which are a logical consequence of the program. We also obtain an important fixpoint characterization of the least Herbrand model.

Proposition 6.1 (Model intersection property)

Let P be a program and $\{M_i\}_{i\in I}$ be a non-empty set of Herbrand models for P. Then $\cap_{i\in I}M_i$ is a Herbrand model for P.

Proof Clearly $\cap_{i\in I}M_i$ is a Herbrand interpretation for P. It is straightforward to show that $\cap_{i\in I}M_i$ is a model for P ∎

Since every program P has B_P as a Herbrand model, the set of all Herbrand models for P is non-empty. Thus the intersection of all Herbrand models for P is again a model, called the *least Herbrand model*, for P. We denote this model by M_P.

The intended interpretation of a program P can, of course, be different from M_P. However, there are very strong reasons for regarding M_P as the canonical interpretation of a program. Certainly, it is usual for the programmer to have in mind the "free" interpretation of the constants and functions in the program given by a Herbrand interpretation. Furthermore, the next theorem shows that the atoms in M_P are precisely those that are logical consequences of the program. This result is due to van Emden and Kowalski [18].

Theorem 6.2 Let P be a program. Then $M_P = \{A\in B_P$: A is a logical

Proof We have that
A is a logical consequence of P
iff $P \cup \{\sim A\}$ is unsatisfiable
iff $P \cup \{\sim A\}$ has no Herbrand models, by proposition 3.3
iff $\sim A$ is false wrt all Herbrand models of P
iff A is true wrt all Herbrand models of P
iff $A \in M_P$ ∎

We wish to obtain a deeper characterization of M_P using fixpoint concepts. For this we need to associate a complete lattice with every program.

Let P be a program. Then 2^{B_P}, which is the set of all Herbrand interpretations of P, is a complete lattice under the partial order of set inclusion $\subseteq$. The top element of this lattice is B_P and the bottom element is $\emptyset$. The least upper bound of any set of Herbrand interpretations is the Herbrand interpretation which is the union of all the Herbrand interpretations in the set. The greatest lower bound is the intersection.

Definition Let P be a program. The mapping $T_P : 2^{B_P} \rightarrow 2^{B_P}$ is defined as follows. Let I be a Herbrand interpretation. Then $T_P(I) = \{A \in B_P : A \leftarrow A_1,...,A_n$ is a ground instance of a clause in P and $\{A_1,...,A_n\} \subseteq I\}$.

The mapping T_P provides the link between the declarative and procedural semantics of P. This definition was first given in [18].

Example Consider the program P
$p(f(x)) \leftarrow p(x)$
$q(a) \leftarrow p(x)$
Put $I_1 = B_P$, $I_2 = T_P(I_1)$ and $I_3 = \emptyset$. Then $T_P(I_1) = \{q(a)\} \cup \{p(f(t)) : t \in U_P\}$, $T_P(I_2) = \{q(a)\} \cup \{p(f(f(t))) : t \in U_P\}$ and $T_P(I_3) = \emptyset$.

Proposition 6.3 Let P be a program. Then the mapping T_P is continuous and, hence, monotonic.

Proof Let X be a directed subset of 2^{B_P}. Note first that $\{A_1,...,A_n\} \subseteq lub(X)$ iff $\{A_1,...,A_n\} \subseteq I$, for some $I \in X$ (see problem 10). In order to show T_P is continuous, we have to show $T_P(lub(X)) = lub(T_P(X))$, for each directed subset X. Now we have that

$A \in T_P(\mathrm{lub}(X))$

iff $A \leftarrow A_1,...,A_n$ is a ground instance of a clause in P and $\{A_1,...,A_n\} \subseteq \mathrm{lub}(X)$

iff $A \leftarrow A_1,...,A_n$ is a ground instance of a clause in P and $\{A_1,...,A_n\} \subseteq I$, for some $I \in X$

iff $A \in T_P(I)$, for some $I \in X$

iff $A \in \mathrm{lub}(T_P(X))$ ∎

Herbrand interpretations which are models can be characterized in terms of T_P.

Proposition 6.4 Let P be a program and I be a Herbrand interpretation of P. Then I is a model for P iff $T_P(I) \subseteq I$.

Proof I is a model for P iff for each ground instance $A \leftarrow A_1,...,A_n$ of each clause in P, we have $\{A_1,...,A_n\} \subseteq I$ implies $A \in I$ iff $T_P(I) \subseteq I$ ∎

Now we come to the first major result of the theory. This theorem, which is due to van Emden and Kowalski [18], provides a fixpoint characterization of the least Herbrand model of a program.

Theorem 6.5 (Fixpoint characterization of least Herbrand model)
Let P be a program. Then $M_P = \mathrm{lfp}(T_P) = T_P\uparrow\omega$.

Proof $M_P = \mathrm{glb}\{I : I \text{ is a Herbrand model for P}\}$
$= \mathrm{glb}\{I : T_P(I) \subseteq I\}$, by proposition 6.4
$= \mathrm{lfp}(T_P)$, by proposition 5.1
$= T_P\uparrow\omega$, by propositions 5.4 and 6.3 ∎

However, it can happen that $\mathrm{gfp}(T_P) \neq T_P\downarrow\omega$.

Example Consider the program P

p(f(x)) ← p(x)

q(a) ← p(x)

Then $T_P\downarrow\omega = \{q(a)\}$, but $\mathrm{gfp}(T_P) = \emptyset$. In fact, $\mathrm{gfp}(T_P) = T_P\downarrow(\omega+1)$.

Theorem 6.2 and the definition of correct answer substitution suggest that we may be able to strengthen theorem 6.2 by showing that an answer substitution θ is correct iff $\forall((A_1 \wedge ... \wedge A_k)\theta)$ is true wrt the least Herbrand hold, as the following example shows.

Example Consider the program P

$p(a) \leftarrow$

Let G be the goal $\leftarrow p(x)$ and θ be the identity substitution. Then $M_P = \{p(a)\}$ and so $\forall x\, p(x)\theta$ is true in M_P. However, θ is not a correct answer substitution, since $\forall x\, p(x)\theta$ is not a logical consequence of P.

The reason for the problem here is that $\sim\forall x\, p(x)$ is not a clause and hence we cannot restrict attention to Herbrand interpretations when attempting to establish the unsatisfiability of $\{p(a)\leftarrow\} \cup \{\sim\forall x\, p(x)\}$. However, if we make a restriction on θ, we do obtain a result which generalizes theorem 6.2.

Theorem 6.6 Let P be a program and G a goal $\leftarrow A_1,\ldots,A_k$. Suppose θ is an answer substitution for $P \cup \{G\}$ such that $(A_1 \wedge \ldots \wedge A_k)\theta$ is ground. Then the following are equivalent:

(a) θ is correct.

(b) $(A_1 \wedge \ldots \wedge A_k)\theta$ is true wrt every Herbrand model of P.

(c) $(A_1 \wedge \ldots \wedge A_k)\theta$ is true wrt the least Herbrand model of P.

Proof Obviously, it suffices to show that (c) implies (a). Now

$(A_1 \wedge \ldots \wedge A_k)\theta$ is true wrt the least Herbrand model of P

implies $(A_1 \wedge \ldots \wedge A_k)\theta$ is true wrt all Herbrand models of P

implies $\sim(A_1 \wedge \ldots \wedge A_k)\theta$ is false wrt all Herbrand models of P

implies $P \cup \{\sim(A_1 \wedge \ldots \wedge A_k)\theta\}$ has no Herbrand models

implies $P \cup \{\sim(A_1 \wedge \ldots \wedge A_k)\theta\}$ has no models, by proposition 3.3 ∎

PROBLEMS FOR CHAPTER 1

1. Consider the formula

$(\forall x\, p(x,x) \wedge \forall x \forall y \forall z\, [(p(x,y) \wedge p(y,z)) \rightarrow p(x,z)] \wedge \forall x \forall y\, [p(x,y) \vee p(y,x)]) \rightarrow \exists y \forall x\, p(y,x)$

(a) Show that every interpretation with a finite domain is a model.

(b) Find an interpretation which is not a model.

2. Complete the proof of proposition 3.2.

3. Suppose θ_1 and θ_2 are substitutions and there exist substitutions σ_1 and σ_2 such that $\theta_1 = \theta_2\sigma_1$ and $\theta_2 = \theta_1\sigma_2$. Show that there exists a variable-pure substitution γ such that $\theta_1 = \theta_2\gamma$.

4. A substitution θ is *idempotent* if $\theta = \theta\theta$. Let $\theta = \{x_1/t_1,\ldots,x_n/t_n\}$ and suppose V is the set of variables occurring in $\{t_1,\ldots,t_n\}$. Show that θ is idempotent iff $\{x_1,\ldots,x_n\} \cap V = \emptyset$.

5. Let θ be a unifier of the finite set S of simple expressions. Prove that θ is an mgu and is idempotent iff for every unifier σ of S, we have $\sigma = \theta\sigma$.

6. For each of the following sets of simple expressions, find mgu's when they exist:

(a) {p(f(y),w,g(z)), p(u,u,v)}

(b) {p(f(y),w,g(z)), p(v,u,v)}

(c) {p(a,x,f(g(y))), p(z,h(z,w),f(w))}

7. Find a complete lattice L and a mapping $T : L \rightarrow L$ such that T is monotonic but not continuous.

8. Complete the proof of proposition 6.1.

9. Find a finite set S of clauses and a non-empty set $\{M_i\}_{i \in I}$ of Herbrand models for S such that $\cap_{i \in I} M_i$ is not a model for S.

10. Let X be a directed subset of the lattice of Herbrand interpretations of a program. Show that $\{A_1,\ldots,A_n\} \subseteq lub(X)$ iff $\{A_1,\ldots,A_n\} \subseteq I$, for some $I \in X$.

11. Let P be the program

p(a) ← p(x), q(x)
p(f(x)) ← p(x)
q(b) ←
q(f(x)) ← q(x)

Show that $T_P\!\downarrow\!\omega = \{p(f^n(a)) : n \in \omega\} \cup \{q(f^n(b)) : n \in \omega\}$ and $gfp(T_P) = T_P\!\downarrow\!\omega 2 = lfp(T_P) = \{q(f^n(b)) : n \in \omega\}$.

12. Let P be the program

q(b) ←

q(f(x)) ← q(x)

p(f(x)) ← p(x)

p(a) ← p(x)

r(c) ← r(x), q(x)

r(f(x)) ← r(x)

Show that $T_P\uparrow\omega = \{q(f^n(b)) : n\in\omega\}$, $T_P\downarrow\omega = \{p(f^n(a) : n\in\omega\} \cup \{q(f^n(b)) : n\in\omega\} \cup \{r(f^n(c)) : n\in\omega\}$ and $T_P\downarrow\omega 2 = \{p(f^n(a)) : n\in\omega\} \cup \{q(f^n(b)) : n\in\omega\} = gfp(T_P)$.

13. Let P be the program

$p_1(f(x)) \leftarrow p_1(x)$

$p_2(a) \leftarrow p_1(x)$

$p_2(f(x)) \leftarrow p_2(x)$

$p_3(a) \leftarrow p_2(x)$

$p_3(f(x)) \leftarrow p_3(x)$

$p_4(a) \leftarrow p_3(x)$

$p_4(f(x)) \leftarrow p_4(x)$

$p_5(a) \leftarrow p_4(x)$

$p_5(f(x)) \leftarrow p_5(x)$

Show that $T_P\downarrow\omega 4 \neq gfp(T_P)$, but $T_P\downarrow\omega 5 = \emptyset = gfp(T_P) = lfp(T_P)$.

14. (a) Let P be a program which contains no function symbols. Show that $T_P\downarrow\omega = gfp(T_P)$.

(b) Let P be a program with the property that, for each clause, each variable in the body of the clause also appears in the head. Show that $T_P\downarrow\omega = gfp(T_P)$.

15. Let P be a program with the following property: for each clause in P, if the clause has variables in the body that do not appear in the head, then the set of variables in the head is disjoint from the set of variables in the body. Prove that $gfp(T_P) = T_P\downarrow\omega n$, for some finite n depending on P.

Chapter 2. PROCEDURAL SEMANTICS

This chapter is concerned with the procedural semantics of logic programs. The procedural counterpart of a correct answer substitution is a computed answer substitution, which is defined using SLD-resolution. We prove that every computed answer substitution is correct and that every correct answer substitution is an instance of a computed answer substitution. This establishes the soundness and completeness of SLD-resolution. The other important result established is the independence of the computation rule. Two pragmatic aspects of PROLOG implementations are also discussed. These are the omission of the occur check from the unification algorithm and the control facility, cut.

§7. SOUNDNESS OF SLD-RESOLUTION

This section introduces the concept of a computed answer substitution and establishes the soundness of SLD-resolution. The implications of omitting the occur check from the unification algorithm are also discussed. While all the requisite results concerning SLD-resolution will be discussed in this and subsequent sections, it would be helpful for the reader to have a wider perspective on automatic theorem proving. We suggest consulting [5], [8], [38] or [39].

There are many refutation procedures based on the resolution inference rule, which are refinements of the original procedure of Robinson [51]. The refutation procedure of interest here has been called *SLD-resolution* in [2]. SLD-resolution stands for SL-resolution for Definite clauses. The SL stands for Linear resolution with Selection function [33]. (The terminology *LUSH-resolution* has also been used [28]). In this and the next two sections, we will procedures.

Definition A *computation rule* is a function from a set of goals to a set of atoms, such that the value of the function for a goal is always an atom, called the *selected* atom, in that goal.

Definition Let G_i be $\leftarrow A_1,\ldots,A_m,\ldots,A_k$, C_{i+1} be $A \leftarrow B_1,\ldots,B_q$ and R be a computation rule. Then G_{i+1} is *derived* from G_i and C_{i+1} using mgu θ_{i+1} via R if the following conditions hold:

(a) A_m is the selected atom given by the computation rule R.

(b) $A_m\theta_{i+1} = A\theta_{i+1}$ (that is, θ_{i+1} is an mgu of A_m and A).

(c) G_{i+1} is the goal $\leftarrow(A_1,\ldots,A_{m-1},B_1,\ldots,B_q,A_{m+1},\ldots,A_k)\theta_{i+1}$.

In resolution terminology, G_{i+1} is a *resolvent* of G_i and C_{i+1}.

Definition Let P be a program, G a goal and R a computation rule. An *SLD-derivation* of $P \cup \{G\}$ via R consists of a (finite or infinite) sequence $G_0=G$, $G_1,\ldots$ of goals, a sequence C_1, $C_2,\ldots$ of variants of program clauses of P and a sequence θ_1, $\theta_2,\ldots$ of mgu's, such that each G_{i+1} is derived from G_i and C_{i+1} using θ_{i+1} via R.

Each C_i is a suitable variant of the corresponding program clause so that C_i does not have any variables which already appear in the derivation up to G_{i-1}. This can be achieved, for example, by subscripting variables in G by 0 and variables in C_i by i. This process of renaming variables is called *standardizing* the variables *apart*. It is necessary, otherwise, for example, we would not be able to unify p(x) and p(f(x)) in $\leftarrow$p(x) and p(f(x))$\leftarrow$. Each program clause variant C_1, $C_2,\ldots$ is called an *input clause* of the derivation.

Definition An *SLD-refutation* of $P \cup \{G\}$ via R is a finite SLD-derivation of $P \cup \{G\}$ via R which has the empty clause $\Box$ as the last goal in the derivation. If $G_n=\Box$, we say the refutation has *length n*.

Throughout this chapter, a "derivation" will always be an "SLD-derivation" and a "refutation" will always be an "SLD-refutation". We can picture SLD-derivations as in Figure 1.

It will be convenient in some of the results to have a slightly more general concept available.

Fig. 1. An SLD-derivation

Definition An *unrestricted SLD-refutation* is an SLD-refutation, except that we drop the requirement that the substitutions θ_i be most general unifiers. They are only required to be unifiers.

SLD-derivations can be *finite* or *infinite*. A finite SLD-derivation can be successful or failed. A *successful* SLD-derivation is one that ends in the empty clause. In other words, a successful derivation is just a refutation. A *failed* SLD-derivation is one that ends in a non-empty goal with the property that the selected atom in this goal does not unify with the head of any program clause. Later we shall see examples of successful, failed and infinite derivations (see Figures 2 and 3).

Definition Let P be a program. The *success set* of P is the set of all $A \in B_P$ such that $P \cup \{\leftarrow A\}$ has an SLD-refutation (using some computation rule depending on A).

The success set is the procedural counterpart of the least Herbrand model. We shall see later that the success set of P is in fact equal to the least Herbrand model of P. Similarly, we have the procedural counterpart of a correct answer substitution.

Definition Let P be a program, G a goal and R a computation rule. An *R-computed answer substitution* θ for $P \cup \{G\}$ is the substitution obtained by restricting the composition $\theta_1 \ldots \theta_n$ to the variables of G, where $\theta_1,\ldots,\theta_n$ is the sequence of mgu's used in an SLD-refutation of $P \cup \{G\}$ via R.

Example If P is the slowsort program, G is the goal ←sort(17.22.6.5.nil,y) and R is any computation rule, then {y/5.6.17.22.nil} is an R-computed answer substitution.

The first soundness result is that R-computed answer substitutions are correct. In the form below, this result is due to Clark [9].

Theorem 7.1 (Soundness of SLD-resolution)
Let P be a program, G a goal and R a computation rule. Then every R-computed answer substitution for $P \cup \{G\}$ is a correct answer substitution.

Proof Let G be the goal $\leftarrow A_1,\ldots,A_k$ and $\theta_1,\ldots,\theta_n$ be the sequence of mgu's used in a refutation of $P \cup \{G\}$ via R. We have to show that $\forall((A_1 \wedge \ldots \wedge A_k)\theta_1 \ldots \theta_n)$ is a logical consequence of P. The result is proved by induction on the length of the refutation.

Suppose first that n=1. This means that G is a goal of the form $\leftarrow A_1$, the program has a unit clause of the form $A\leftarrow$ and $A_1\theta_1 = A\theta_1$. Since $A_1\theta_1$ is an instance of a unit clause of P, it follows that $\forall(A_1\theta_1)$ is a logical consequence of P.

Next suppose that the result holds for R-computed answer substitutions which come from refutations of length n-1. Suppose $\theta_1,...,\theta_n$ is the sequence of mgu's used in a refutation of $P \cup \{G\}$ of length n. Let $A\leftarrow B_1,...,B_q$ $(q\geq 0)$ be the first input clause and A_m the selected atom of G. By the induction hypothesis, $\forall((A_1\wedge...\wedge A_{m-1}\wedge B_1\wedge...\wedge B_q\wedge A_{m+1}\wedge...\wedge A_k)\theta_1...\theta_n)$ is a logical consequence of P. Thus, if $q>0$, $\forall((B_1\wedge...\wedge B_q)\theta_1...\theta_n)$ is a logical consequence of P. Consequently, $\forall(A_m\theta_1...\theta_n) = \forall(A\theta_1...\theta_n)$ is a logical consequence of P. Hence $\forall((A_1\wedge...\wedge A_k)\theta_1...\theta_n)$ is a logical consequence of P ∎

Corollary 7.2 Let P be a program, G a goal and R a computation rule. Suppose there exists an SLD-refutation of $P \cup \{G\}$ via R. Then $P \cup \{G\}$ is unsatisfiable.

Proof Let G be the goal $\leftarrow A_1,...,A_k$. By theorem 7.1, the R-computed answer substitution θ coming from the refutation is correct. Thus $\forall((A_1\wedge...\wedge A_k)\theta)$ is a logical consequence of P. It follows that $P \cup \{G\}$ is unsatisfiable ∎

Corollary 7.3 The success set of a program is contained in its least Herbrand model.

Proof Let the program be P, let $A\in B_P$ and suppose $P \cup \{\leftarrow A\}$ has a refutation via some computation rule. By theorem 7.1, A is a logical consequence of P. Thus, by theorem 6.2, A is in the least Herbrand model of P ∎

It is possible to be more precise than corollary 7.3. We can show that if $A\in B_P$ and $P \cup \{\leftarrow A\}$ has a refutation of length n, then $A\in T_P\uparrow n$. This result is due to Apt and van Emden [2].

If A is an atom, we put $[A] = \{A'\in B_P : A'=A\theta$, for some substitution $\theta\}$. Thus [A] is the set of all ground instances of A.

Theorem 7.4 Let P be a program, G a goal $\leftarrow A_1,...,A_k$ and R a computation rule. Suppose that $P \cup \{G\}$ has an SLD-refutation of length n via R and $\theta_1,\ldots,\theta_n$ is the sequence of mgu's of the SLD-refutation. Then we have that $\cup_{j=1}^{k}[A_j\theta_1\ldots\theta_n] \subseteq T_P\uparrow n$.

Proof The result is proved by induction on the length of the refutation. Suppose first that n=1. Then G is a goal of the form $\leftarrow A_1$, the program has a unit clause of the form $A\leftarrow$ and $A_1\theta_1 = A\theta_1$. Clearly, $[A] \subseteq T_P\uparrow 1$ and so $[A_1\theta_1] \subseteq T_P\uparrow 1$.

Next suppose the result is true for refutations of length n–1 and consider a refutation of $P \cup \{G\}$ of length n. Let A_j be an atom of G. Suppose first that A_j is not the selected atom of G. Thus $A_j\theta_1$ is an atom of G_1, the second goal of the refutation. The induction hypothesis implies that $[A_j\theta_1\theta_2\ldots\theta_n] \subseteq T_P\uparrow(n-1)$ and $T_P\uparrow(n-1) \subseteq T_P\uparrow n$, by the monotonicity of T_P.

Now suppose that A_j is the selected atom of G. Let $B\leftarrow B_1,\ldots,B_q$ $(q\geq 0)$ be the first input clause. Thus $A_j\theta_1$ is an instance of B. If q=0, we have $[B] \subseteq T_P\uparrow 1$. Thus $[A_j\theta_1\ldots\theta_n] \subseteq [A_j\theta_1] \subseteq [B] \subseteq T_P\uparrow 1 \subseteq T_P\uparrow n$. If q>0, by the induction hypothesis, $[B_i\theta_1\ldots\theta_n] \subseteq T_P\uparrow(n-1)$, for i=1,...,q. By the definition of T_P, we have that $[A_j\theta_1\ldots\theta_n] \subseteq T_P\uparrow n$ ∎

Next we turn to the problem of the occur check. As we mentioned earlier, the occur check in the unification algorithm is very expensive and most PROLOG systems leave it out for the pragmatic reason that it is only very rarely required. While this is certainly true, its omission can cause serious difficulties.

Example Consider the program

test ← p(x,x)

p(x,f(x)) ←

Given the goal ←test, a PROLOG system without the occur check will answer "yes" (equivalently, ϵ is a correct answer substitution)! This answer is quite wrong because test is not a logical consequence of the program. The problem arises because, without the occur check, the unification algorithm of the PROLOG system will mistakenly unify p(x,x) and p(y,f(y)).

Thus we see that the lack of occur check has destroyed one of the principles on which logic programming is based – the soundness of SLD-resolution.

Example Consider the program

test ← p(x,x)

p(x,f(x)) ← p(x,x)

This time a PROLOG system without the occur check will go into an infinite loop in the unification algorithm because it will attempt to use a "circular" binding made in the second step of the computation.

These examples illustrate what can go wrong. We can distinguish two cases. The first case is when a circular binding is constructed in a "unification", but this binding is never used again. The first example illustrates this. The second case happens when an attempt is made to use a previously constructed circular binding in a step of the computation or in printing out an answer. The second example illustrates this. The first case is more insidious because there may be no indication that an error has occurred.

While these examples may appear artificial, it is important to appreciate that we can easily have such behaviour in practical programs. The most common situation where this can occur is when programming with difference lists [14]. A difference list is a term of the form x–y, where – is a binary function (written infix). x–y represents the difference between the two lists x and y. For example, 34.56.12.x–x represents the list [34, 56, 12]. Similarly, x–x represents the empty list.

Let us say two difference lists x–y and z–w are compatible if y=z. Then compatible difference lists can be concatenated in constant time using the definition [14]

concat(x–y,y–z,x–z) ←

For example, we can concatenate 12.34.67.45.x–x and 36.89.y–y in one step to obtain 12.34.67.45.36.89.z–z. This is clearly a very useful technique. However, it is also dangerous in the absence of the occur check.

Example Consider the program

test ← concat(u–u,v–v,a.w–w)

concat(x–y,y–z,x–z) ←

Given the goal ←test, a PROLOG system without the occur check will answer "yes". In other words, it thinks that the concatenation of the empty list with the empty list is the list [a]!

Programs which use the difference list technique normally do not have an explicit concat predicate. Instead the concatenation is done implicitly. For example, the following clause is taken from such a version of quicksort [54].

Example Consider the program

qsort(nil,x–x) ←

Given the goal ←qsort(nil,a.y–y), a PROLOG system without the occur check will succeed on the goal (however, it will have a problem printing out its "answer", which contains the circular binding y/a.y).

It is possible to minimize the danger of an occur check problem by using a certain programming methodology. The idea is to "protect" programs which could cause problems by putting an appropriate top-level predicate to restrict uses of the program to those which are known to be sound. This means that there must be some mechanism for forcing all calls to the program to go through this top-level predicate. However, with this method, the onus is still on the programmer and it thus remains suspect. A better idea [49] is to have a preprocessor which is able to identify which clauses may cause problems and add checking code to these clauses (or perhaps invoke the full unification algorithm when these clauses are used).

§8. COMPLETENESS OF SLD-RESOLUTION

The major result of this section is the completeness of SLD-resolution. We begin with two very useful lemmas.

Lemma 8.1 (mgu lemma)

Let P be a program and G be a goal. Suppose that $P \cup \{G\}$ has an unrestricted SLD-refutation. Then $P \cup \{G\}$ has an SLD-refutation of the same length. Furthermore, if $\theta_1,\ldots,\theta_n$ are the unifiers from the unrestricted SLD-refutation and $\theta'_1,\ldots,\theta'_n$ are the mgu's from the SLD-refutation, then there exists a substitution γ such that $\theta_1\ldots\theta_n = \theta'_1\ldots\theta'_n\gamma$.

Proof The proof is by induction on the length of the unrestricted refutation. Suppose first that n=1. Thus $P \cup \{G\}$ has an unrestricted refutation G_0=G, G_1=□ with input clause C_1 and unifier θ_1. Suppose θ'_1 is an mgu of the atom in G and the head of the unit clause C_1. Then $\theta_1 = \theta'_1\gamma$, for some γ. Furthermore, $P \cup \{G\}$ has a refutation G_0=G, G_1=□ with input clause C_1 and mgu θ_1'.

Now suppose the result holds for n–1. Suppose $P \cup \{G\}$ has an unrestricted refutation $G_0=G$, $G_1,...,G_n=\Box$ of length n with input clauses $C_1,...,C_n$ and unifiers $\theta_1,...,\theta_n$. There exists an mgu θ_1' for the selected atom in G and the head of C_1 such that $\theta_1 = \theta_1'\rho$, for some ρ. Thus $P \cup \{G\}$ has an unrestricted refutation $G_0=G$, G_1', $G_2,...,G_n=\Box$ with input clauses $C_1,...,C_n$ and unifiers θ_1', $\rho\theta_2$, $\theta_3,...,\theta_n$, where $G_1 = G_1'\rho$. By the induction hypothesis, $P \cup \{G_1'\}$ has a refutation G_1', $G_2',...,G_n'=\Box$ with mgu's $\theta_2',...,\theta_n'$ such that $\rho\theta_2...\theta_n = \theta_2'...\theta_n'\gamma$, for some γ. Thus $P \cup \{G\}$ has a refutation $G_0=G$, $G_1',...,G_n'=\Box$ with mgu's $\theta_1',...,\theta_n'$ such that $\theta_1...\theta_n = \theta_1'\rho\theta_2...\theta_n = \theta_1'...\theta_n'\gamma$ ∎

Lemma 8.2 (Lifting lemma)

Let P be a program, G a goal and θ a substitution. Suppose there exists an SLD-refutation of $P \cup \{G\theta\}$. Then there exists an SLD-refutation of $P \cup \{G\}$ of the same length. Furthermore, if $\theta_1,...,\theta_n$ are the mgu's from the SLD-refutation of $P \cup \{G\theta\}$ and $\theta_1',...,\theta_n'$ are the mgu's from the SLD-refutation of $P \cup \{G\}$, then there exists a substitution γ such that $\theta\theta_1...\theta_n = \theta_1'...\theta_n'\gamma$.

Proof Suppose the first input clause for the refutation of $P \cup \{G\theta\}$ is C_1, the first mgu is θ_1 and G_1 is the goal which results from the first step. We may assume θ does not act on any variables of C_1. Now $\theta\theta_1$ is a unifier for the head of C_1 and the atom in G which corresponds to the selected atom in $G\theta$. The result of resolving G and C_1 using $\theta\theta_1$ is exactly G_1. Thus we obtain an unrestricted refutation of $P \cup \{G\}$, which looks exactly like the given refutation of $P \cup \{G\theta\}$, except the original goal is different, of course, and the first unifier is $\theta\theta_1$. Now apply the mgu lemma ∎

The first completeness result gives the converse to corollary 7.3. This result is due to Apt and van Emden [2].

Theorem 8.3 The success set of a program is equal to its least Herbrand model.

Proof Let the program be P. By corollary 7.3, it suffices to show that the least Herbrand model of P is contained in the success set of P. Suppose A is in the least Herbrand model of P. By theorem 6.5, $A \in T_P \uparrow n$, for some $n \in \omega$. We prove by induction on n that $A \in T_P \uparrow n$ implies that $P \cup \{\leftarrow A\}$ has a

Suppose first that n=1. Then $A \in T_P \uparrow 1$ means that A is a ground instance of a unit clause of P. Clearly, $P \cup \{\leftarrow A\}$ has a refutation.

Now suppose that the result holds for n-1. Let $A \in T_P \uparrow n$. By the definition of T_P, there exists a ground instance of a clause $B \leftarrow B_1,\ldots,B_k$ such that $A = B\theta$ and $\{B_1\theta,\ldots,B_k\theta\} \subseteq T_P \uparrow (n-1)$, for some θ. By the induction hypothesis, $P \cup \{\leftarrow B_i\theta\}$ has a refutation, for i=1,...,k. Because each $B_i\theta$ is ground, these refutations can be combined into a refutation of $P \cup \{\leftarrow (B_1,\ldots,B_k)\theta\}$. Thus $P \cup \{\leftarrow A\}$ has an unrestricted refutation and we can apply the mgu lemma to obtain a refutation of $P \cup \{\leftarrow A\}$ ▮

The next completeness result was first proved by Hill [28]. See also [2].

Theorem 8.4 Let P be a program and G a goal. Suppose that $P \cup \{G\}$ is unsatisfiable. Then there exists a computation rule R and an SLD-refutation of $P \cup \{G\}$ via R.

Proof Let G be the goal $\leftarrow A_1,\ldots,A_k$. Since $P \cup \{G\}$ is unsatisfiable, G is false wrt M_P. Hence some ground instance $G\theta$ of G is false wrt M_P. Thus $\{A_1\theta,\ldots,A_k\theta\} \subseteq M_P$. By theorem 8.3, there is a refutation for $P \cup \{\leftarrow A_i\theta\}$, for i=1,...,k. Since each $A_i\theta$ is ground, we can combine these refutations into a refutation for $P \cup \{G\theta\}$. Finally, we apply the lifting lemma ▮

Next we turn attention to correct answer substitutions. It is not possible to prove the exact converse of theorem 7.1 because computed answer substitutions are always "most general". However, we can prove that every correct answer substitution is an instance of a computed answer substitution.

Lemma 8.5 Let P be a program and A an atom. Suppose that $\forall(A)$ is a logical consequence of P. Then there exists an SLD-refutation of $P \cup \{\leftarrow A\}$ with the identity substitution as the computed answer substitution.

Proof Suppose A has variables $x_1,\ldots,x_n$. Let $a_1,\ldots,a_n$ be distinct constants not appearing in P or A and let θ be the substitution $\{x_1/a_1,\ldots,x_n/a_n\}$. Then it is clear that $A\theta$ is a logical consequence of P. Since $A\theta$ is ground, theorem 8.3 shows that $P \cup \{\leftarrow A\theta\}$ has a refutation. Since the a_i do not appear in P or A, by textually replacing a_i by x_i (i=1,...,n) in this refutation, we obtain a refutation of $P \cup \{\leftarrow A\}$ with the identity substitution as the computed answer substitution ▮

Now we are in a position to prove the major completeness result. This result is due to Clark [9].

Theorem 8.6 (Completeness of SLD-resolution)

Let P be a program and G a goal. For every correct answer substitution θ for $P \cup \{G\}$, there exists a computation rule R, an R-computed answer substitution σ for $P \cup \{G\}$ and a substitution γ such that $\theta = \sigma\gamma$.

Proof Suppose G is the goal $\leftarrow A_1,...,A_k$. Since θ is correct, $\forall((A_1 \wedge ... \wedge A_k)\theta)$ is a logical consequence of P. By lemma 8.5, there exists a refutation of $P \cup \{\leftarrow A_i\theta\}$ such that the computed answer substitution is the identity, for i=1,...,k. We can combine these refutations into a refutation of $P \cup \{G\theta\}$ such that the computed answer substitution is the identity.

Suppose the sequence of mgu's of the refutation of $P \cup \{G\theta\}$ is $\theta_1,...,\theta_n$. Then $G\theta\theta_1...\theta_n = G\theta$. By the lifting lemma, there exists a refutation of $P \cup \{G\}$ with mgu's $\theta_1',...,\theta_n'$ such that $\theta\theta_1...\theta_n = \theta_1'...\theta_n'\gamma'$, for some substitution γ'. Let σ be $\theta_1'...\theta_n'$ restricted to the variables in G. Then $\theta = \sigma\gamma$, where γ is an appropriate restriction of γ' ∎

§9. INDEPENDENCE OF THE COMPUTATION RULE

Theorem 8.4 shows that if $P \cup \{G\}$ is unsatisfiable, then there exists a refutation of $P \cup \{G\}$ using some computation rule R, say. However, so far, R is not under our control. The results of this section show that the computation rule can be specified in advance and then if $P \cup \{G\}$ is unsatisfiable, we can always find a refutation using the given computation rule. This fact is called the "independence" of the computation rule. It has important implications for logic programming systems, which we will explore in §10.

The key to the independence result is a technical lemma. For this, it will be convenient to introduce some new notation. If C is a program clause, then C^+ denotes the head of the clause and C^- denotes the body.

Lemma 9.1 (Switching lemma)

Let P be a program, G a goal and R a computation rule. Suppose that

$P \cup \{G\}$ has an SLD-refutation $G = G, G, ..., G, G, ..., G = \Box$ with

G_{q-1} is $\leftarrow A_1,\ldots,A_{i-1},A_i,\ldots,A_{j-1},A_j,\ldots,A_k$

G_q is $\leftarrow(A_1,\ldots,A_{i-1},C_q^-,\ldots,A_{j-1},A_j,\ldots,A_k)\theta_q$

G_{q+1} is $\leftarrow(A_1,\ldots,A_{i-1},C_q^-,\ldots,A_{j-1},C_{q+1}^-,\ldots,A_k)\theta_q\theta_{q+1}$.

Then there exists an SLD-refutation of $P \cup \{G\}$ using the computation rule R', which is the same as R except that A_j is selected in G_{q-1} instead of A_i and A_i is selected in G_q instead of A_j. Furthermore, if σ is the R-computed answer substitution for $P \cup \{G\}$ and σ' is the R'-computed answer substitution, then $G\sigma$ is a variant of $G\sigma'$.

Proof We have $A_j\theta_q\theta_{q+1} = C_{q+1}^+\theta_{q+1} = C_{q+1}^+\theta_q\theta_{q+1}$. Thus we can unify A_j and C_{q+1}^+. Let θ_q' be an mgu of A_j and C_{q+1}^+. Thus $\theta_q\theta_{q+1} = \theta_q'\sigma$, for some substitution σ. Clearly, θ_q' does not act on any of the variables of C_q.

Furthermore, $C_q^+\sigma = C_q^+\theta_q'\sigma = C_q^+\theta_q\theta_{q+1} = A_i\theta_q\theta_{q+1} = A_i\theta_q'\sigma$. Hence we can unify C_q^+ and $A_i\theta_q'$. Suppose θ_{q+1}' is an mgu. Thus $\sigma = \theta_{q+1}'\sigma'$, for some σ'. Consequently, $\theta_q\theta_{q+1} = \theta_q'\theta_{q+1}'\sigma'$. We have now shown that A_i and A_j can be selected in the reverse order.

Next, note that $A_i\theta_q'\theta_{q+1}' = C_q^+\theta_q'\theta_{q+1}'$, but that θ_q is an mgu of A_i and C_q^+. Thus $\theta_q'\theta_{q+1}' = \theta_q\gamma$, for some γ. But $A_j\theta_q\gamma = A_j\theta_q'\theta_{q+1}' = C_{q+1}^+\theta_q'\theta_{q+1}' = C_{q+1}^+\theta_q\gamma = C_{q+1}^+\gamma$. Thus γ unifies $A_j\theta_q$ and C_{q+1}^+, and so $\gamma = \theta_{q+1}\sigma''$, for some σ''. Consequently, $\theta_q'\theta_{q+1}' = \theta_q\theta_{q+1}\sigma''$ and so the (q+1)th goal in the refutation via R' is a variant of G_{q+1}.

The remainder of the refutation via R' now proceeds in the same way as via R (modulo variants) and the result follows ∎

Theorem 9.2 (Independence of the computation rule).

Let P be a program, G a goal and R a computation rule. Suppose there is an SLD-refutation of $P \cup \{G\}$ via R. Let R' be any computation rule. Then there exists an SLD-refutation of $P \cup \{G\}$ via R'. Furthermore, if σ and σ' are the respective computed answer substitutions, then $G\sigma$ is a variant of $G\sigma'$.

Proof Apply the switching lemma repeatedly. (The details are left to problem 6) ∎

We can use theorem 9.2 to strengthen theorems 8.3, 8.4 and 8.6.

Definition Let P be a program and R a computation rule. The *R-success set* of P is the set of all $A \in B_P$ such that $P \cup \{\leftarrow A\}$ has an SLD-refutation via R.

Theorem 9.3 Let P be a program and R a computation rule. Then the R-success set of P is equal to its least Herbrand model.

Proof The theorem follows immediately from theorems 8.3 and 9.2 ∎

Theorem 9.4 Let P be a program, G a goal and R a computation rule. Suppose that $P \cup \{G\}$ is unsatisfiable. Then there exists an SLD-refutation of $P \cup \{G\}$ via R.

Proof The theorem follows immediately from theorems 8.4 and 9.2 ∎

Theorem 9.5 (Strong completeness of SLD-resolution)
Let P be a program, G a goal and R a computation rule. Then for every correct answer substitution θ for $P \cup \{G\}$, there exists an R-computed answer substitution σ for $P \cup \{G\}$ and a substitution γ such that $\theta = \sigma\gamma$.

Proof The theorem follows immediately from theorems 8.6 and 9.2 ∎

Theorem 9.4 is due to Hill [28]. See also [2]. Theorem 9.5 is due to Clark [9]. These results built on earlier completeness results described in [38].

§10. SLD-REFUTATION PROCEDURES

In this section, we consider the possible strategies a logic programming system might adopt in its search for a refutation. We show that the use of a depth-first search strategy has serious implications with regard to completeness. We also briefly discuss the automatic generation of control.

The search space is a certain type of tree, called an SLD-tree. The results of §9 show that in building the SLD-tree, the system does not have to advance and an SLD-tree constructed using this computation rule. This dramatically reduces the size of the search space.

Definition Let P be a program, G a goal and R a computation rule. Then the *SLD-tree* for P ∪ {G} via R is defined as follows:

(a) Each node of the tree is a goal (possibly empty).

(b) The root node is G.

(c) Let $\leftarrow A_1,\dots,A_m,\dots,A_k$ $(k \geq 1)$ be a node in the tree and suppose that A_m is the atom selected by R. Then this node has a descendent for each input clause $A \leftarrow B_1,\dots,B_q$ such that A_m and A are unifiable. The descendent is

$$\leftarrow (A_1,\dots,A_{m-1},B_1,\dots,B_q,A_{m+1},\dots,A_k)\theta$$

where θ is an mgu of A_m and A.

(d) Nodes which are the empty clause have no descendents.

Each branch of the SLD-tree is a derivation of P ∪ {G}. Branches corresponding to successful derivations are called *success branches*, branches corresponding to infinite derivations are called *infinite branches* and branches corresponding to failed derivations are called *failure branches.*

Example Consider the program

1. $p(x,z) \leftarrow q(x,y), p(y,z)$
2. $p(x,x) \leftarrow$
3. $q(a,b) \leftarrow$

and the goal $\leftarrow p(x,b)$. Figures 2 and 3 show two SLD-trees for this program and goal. The SLD-tree in Figure 2 comes from the standard PROLOG computation rule (select the leftmost atom). The SLD-tree in Figure 3 comes from the computation rule which always selects the rightmost atom. The selected atoms are underlined and the success, failure and infinite branches are shown. Note that the first tree is finite, while the second tree is infinite. Each tree has two success branches corresponding to the answers {x/a} and {x/b}.

This example shows that the choice of computation rule has a great bearing on the size and structure of the corresponding SLD-tree. However, no matter what the choice of computation rule, if P ∪ {G} is unsatisfiable, then the corresponding SLD-tree does have a success branch. This is just a restatement of theorem 9.4.

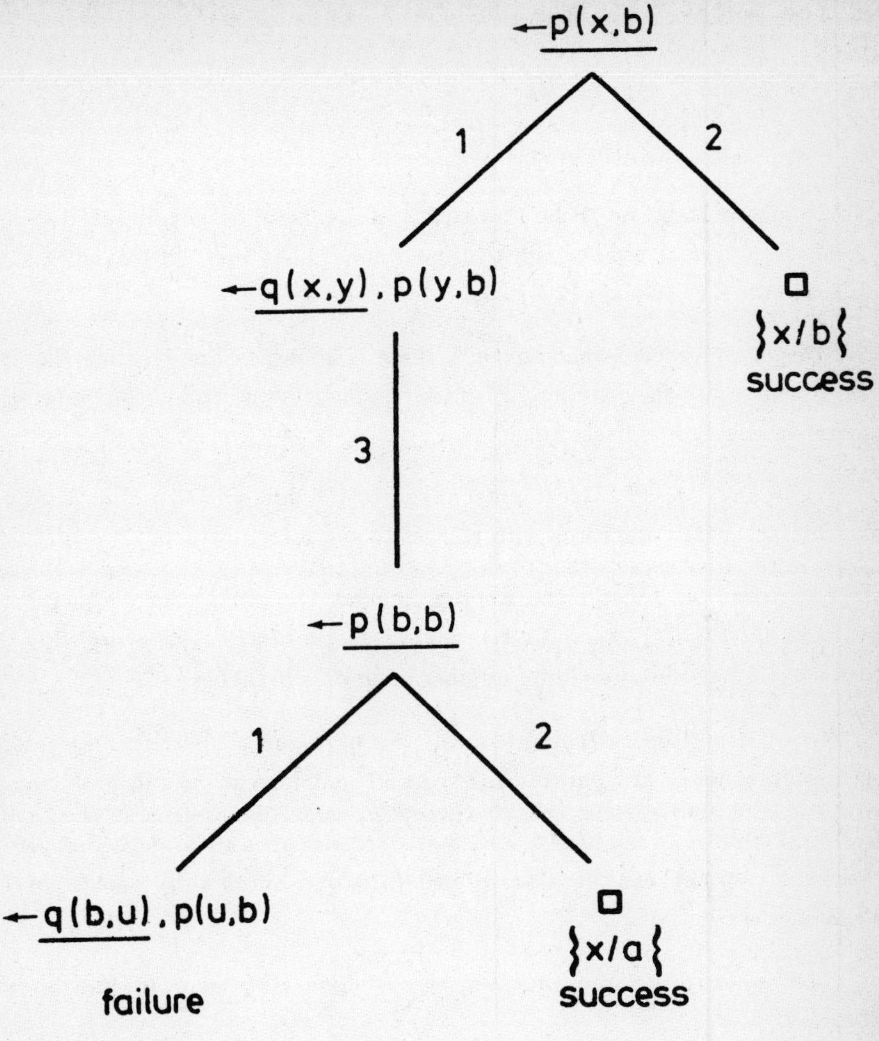

Fig. 2. A finite SLD-tree

Theorem 10.1 Let P be a program, G a goal and R a computation rule. Suppose that P ∪ {G} is unsatisfiable. Then the SLD-tree for P ∪ {G} via R has at least one success branch.

Theorem 9.5 can also be restated.

Theorem 10.2 Let P be a program, G a goal and R a computation rule. Then every correct answer substitution θ for P ∪ {G} is "displayed" on the SLD-tree for P ∪ {G} via R.

"Displayed" means that, given θ, there is a success branch such that θ is an instance of the computed answer substitution from the refutation corresponding to this branch.

While any two SLD-trees may have greatly different size and structure, they are essentially the same with respect to success branches.

Theorem 10.3 Let P be a program and G a goal. Then either every SLD-tree for P ∪ {G} has infinitely many success branches or every SLD-tree for P ∪ {G} has the same finite number of success branches.

Proof Using the switching lemma, we can set up a bijection between the success branches of any pair of SLD-trees. (The details are left to problem 8) ∎

For example, in Figures 2 and 3, the respective success branches giving the answer {x/a} can be transformed into one another by means of the switching lemma.

Next we turn to the problem of searching SLD-trees to find success branches.

Definition A *search rule* is a strategy for searching SLD-trees to find success branches. An *SLD-refutation procedure* is specified by a computation rule together with a search rule.

Standard PROLOG systems employ the computation rule which always selects the leftmost atom in a goal together with a depth-first search rule. The search rule is implemented by means of a stack of goals. An instance of the goal stack represents the branch currently being investigated. The computation essentially becomes an interleaved sequence of pushes and pops on this stack. A push occurs when the selected atom in the goal at the top of

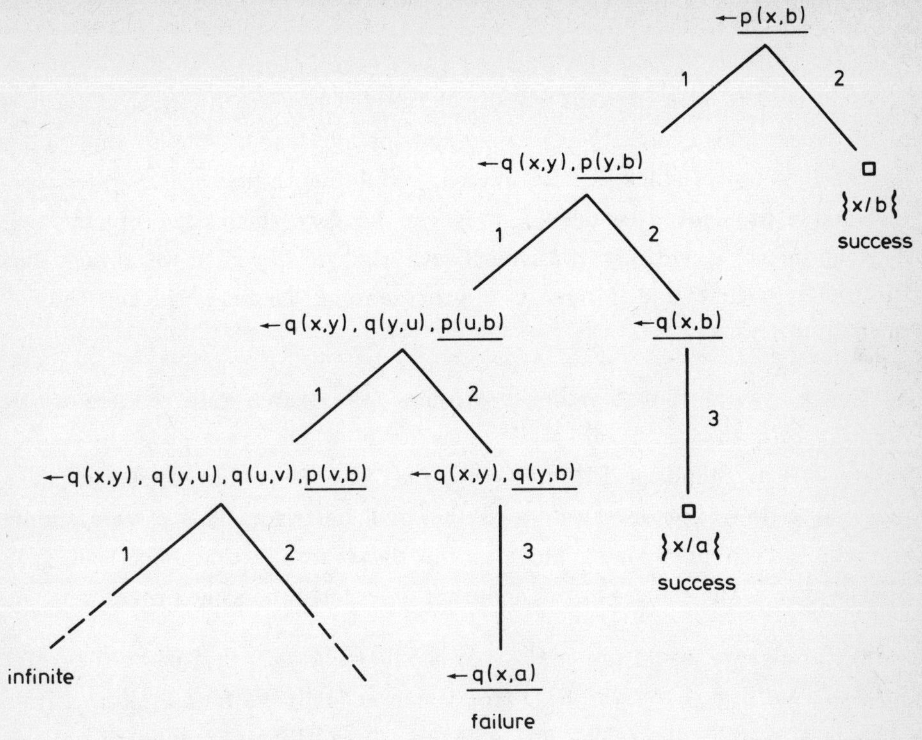

Fig. 3. An infinite SLD-tree

the stack is successfully unified with the head of a program clause. The resolvent is pushed onto the stack. A pop occurs when there are no (more) program clauses with head to match the selected atom in the goal at the top of the stack. This goal is then popped and the next choice of matching clause for the new top of stack is investigated. While depth-first search rules have undeniable problems (see below), they can be very efficiently implemented. This approach is entirely consistent with the view, which we share, that PROLOG is first and foremost a programming language rather than a theorem prover.

For a system that searches depth-first, the search rule reduces to an *ordering rule*, that is, a rule which specifies in which order program clauses will be tried. Standard PROLOG systems use the order of clauses in a program as the fixed order in which they will be tried. This is very simple and efficient to implement, but has the disadvantage that each call to a definition tries the clauses in the definition in exactly the same order.

Naturally, we would prefer the search rule to be *fair*, that is, be such that each success branch on the SLD-tree will eventually be found. For infinite SLD-trees, search rules which do not have a breadth-first component are not likely to be fair. However, a breadth-first component is less compatible with an efficient implementation.

Let us now consider the "completeness" of logic programming systems that use a depth-first search rule combined with a fixed try order of clauses given by their ordering in the program. As well as standard PROLOG systems, let us also consider systems, such as IC-PROLOG [13] and MU-PROLOG [45], [46], which allow more complex computation rules. According to theorem 10.1, if $P \cup \{G\}$ is unsatisfiable, no matter what the computation rule, the corresponding SLD-tree always contains a success branch. The question is this: will logic programming systems with a depth-first search rule using a fixed try order of program clauses and an arbitrary computation rule, guarantee to always find the success branch? Unfortunately, the answer is no. In other words, none of the earlier completeness results is applicable to most current PROLOG systems because efficiency considerations have forced the implementation of unfair search rules!

Let us consider an example to make this clear.

Example Let P be the program

1. p(a,b) ←
2. p(c,b) ←
3. p(x,z) ← p(x,y), p(y,z)
4. p(x,y) ← p(y,x)

and G be the goal ←p(a,c). It is straightforward to show that P ∪ {G} has a refutation and, moreover, that if any clause of P is omitted, P ∪ {G} will no longer have a refutation.

We claim that no matter how the clauses of P are ordered and no matter what the computation rule, a logic programming system using a depth-first search with the fixed try order of program clauses, will never find a refutation.

This claim follows immediately from the fact that clauses 3 and 4 have completely general heads. Hence they will always match any subgoal. Thus if clause 3 is before clause 4 in the program, the system will never consider clause 4 and vice versa. However, all clauses are needed in any refutation.

Figure 4 illustrates the situation. There we have given the SLD-tree resulting from the use of the standard computation rule, which selects the leftmost atom, and the try order of clauses given by the order of the clauses in the above program. As can be seen, the leftmost branch of this SLD-tree is infinite and thus a depth-first search will never find the success branch. In fact, for every computation rule and every fixed try order of the program clauses, the leftmost branch of the corresponding SLD-tree is infinite.

Finally, we discuss the importance of using appropriate computation rules. Recall that one of the major problems in logic programming research is the control problem. It would clearly be a substantial step towards the solution of this problem if we were able to build systems with the ability to autonomously find an appropriate computation rule for each program run on the system. To illustrate what is involved in this, consider once again the slowsort program.

sort(x,y) ← sorted(y), perm(x,y)
sorted(nil) ←
sorted(x.nil) ←
sorted(x.y.z) ← x≤y, sorted(y.z)
perm(nil,nil) ←
perm(x.y,u.v) ← delete(u,x.y,z), perm(z,v)

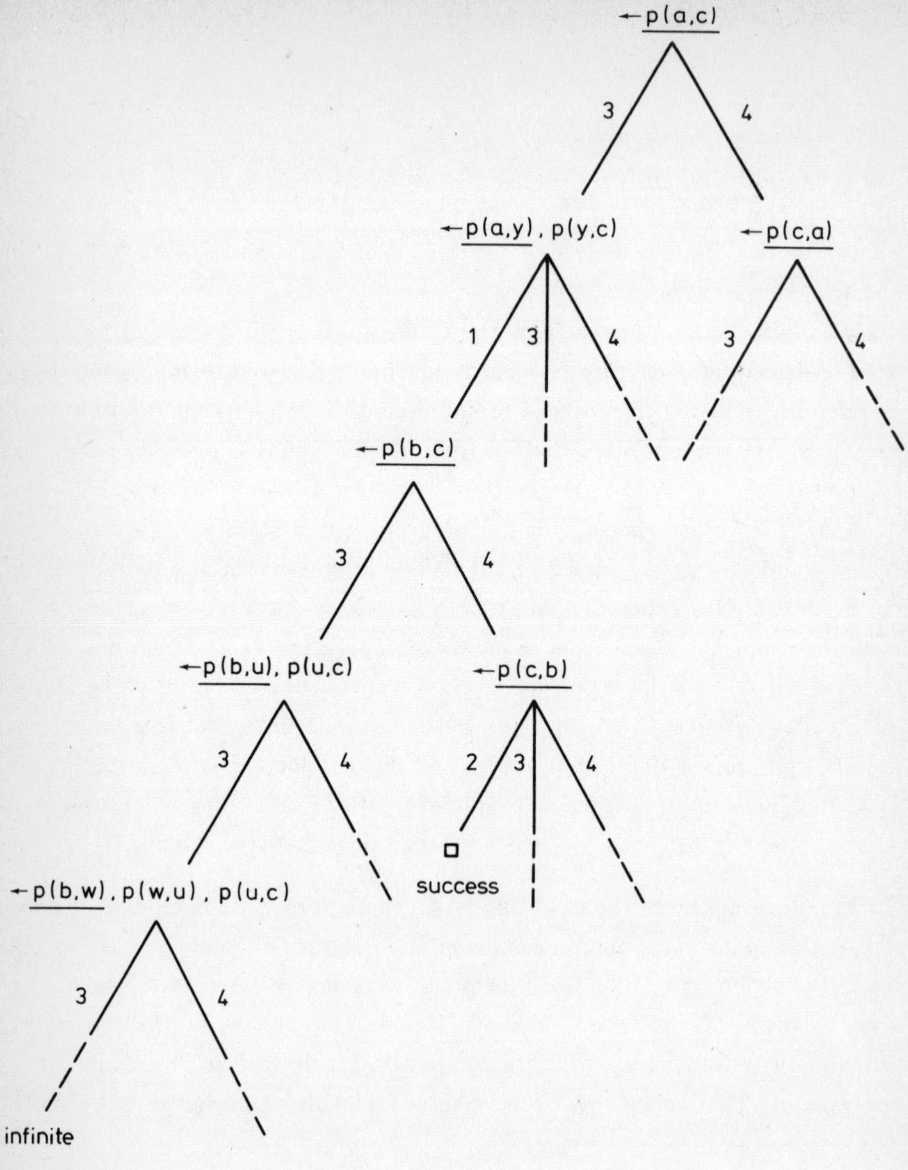

Fig. 4. SLD-tree which illustrates problem with depth-first search

delete(x,y.z,y.w) ← delete(x,z,w)

$0 \leq x$ ←

$f(x) \leq f(y)$ ← $x \leq y$

Now the first thing to note about slowsort is that it does not run on standard PROLOG systems! Consider the goal ←sort(17.22.6.5.nil,y). A standard PROLOG system goes into an infinite loop because sorted makes longer and longer incorrect guesses for y. Of course, sorted has no business guessing at all. It is purely a test. Thus a way to fix the problem is to change the definition of sort to

sort(x,y) ← perm(x,y), sorted(y)

This at least gives a program which runs, even if it is spectacularly inefficient. It sorts the given list by making random permutations of it and then using sorted to check if the permutations are sorted.

The attraction of the slowsort program is that it does give a very clear logic component for a sorting program. The disadvantage for standard PROLOG systems is that the only way to make it reasonably efficient is to substantially change the logic. To keep the above simple logic what we require is a computation rule which coroutines between perm and sorted. Thus the list is given to perm which generates a *partial* permutation of it and then checks with sorted to see if the partial permutation is correct so far. If sorted finds that the partial permutation is sorted, perm generates a bit more of the permutation and then checks with sorted again. Otherwise, perm undoes a bit of the partial permutation, generates a slightly different partial permutation and checks with sorted again. Such a program is clearly going to be a great deal more efficient than the one which generates an entire permutation before checking to see if it is sorted.

Thus we can obtain a more efficient sorting program by adding clever control to the simple logic. (Of course, much more efficient sorting programs are known, but this is not the point of the discussion). There are now a number of PROLOG systems which allow the programmer to specify such control. For example, in MU-PROLOG the programmer would add the wait declaration

?- wait sorted(0)

to the program. The argument 0 means that when sorted is called it is not constructed if a variable in it is bound to a non-variable). If a call to sorted constructs the argument in the subgoal, then the subgoal is delayed. The offending variables are marked and when any of them are bound later, the delayed subgoal is resumed. This simple mechanism achieves precisely the desired behaviour.

In standard PROLOG systems, a "generate" subgoal should come before a "test" subgoal. Thus perm should be put before sorted, if slowsort is to be run on a standard PROLOG system. However, in MU-PROLOG, the "test" should be put before the "generate". This order together with appropriate wait declarations on the "test" ensure the proper coroutining between the "test" and the "generate". The coroutining starts by delaying the "test". The "generate" is then run until it creates a binding which causes the "test" to be resumed, and so on.

Wait declarations would not be of major interest if their addition always required programmer intervention. However, MU-PROLOG has a preprocessor which is able to *automatically* add wait declarations to many programs in order to obtain more sensible behaviour. For example, given the slowsort program as input, the preprocessor outputs the above wait declaration for sorted. (It also gives wait declarations for perm, delete and $\leq$, but these are not needed for the use we have made of slowsort). It does this by finding clauses with recursive calls which could cause infinite loops and generating sufficient wait declarations to stop the loops. The preprocessor is also able to recognize that sorted is a "test" and should appear before perm in the first clause. It will reorder sorted and perm, if necessary. A detailed account of the automatic generation of control is given in [46]. By relieving programmers of some of the responsibility for providing control in this way, MU-PROLOG is thus a step towards the solution of the control problem.

§11. CUTS

In this section, we discuss the cut, which is a widely used and controversial control facility offered by PROLOG systems. It is usually written as "!" in programs, although some systems call it slash and write it as "/". There has been considerable discussion of the advantages and disadvantages of cut and, in particular, whether it "affects the semantics" of programs in which it appears. We argue that cut does *not* affect the declarative semantics of programs, but it can introduce an undesirable form of incompleteness into the refutation procedure.

First, we must be precise about what a cut actually does. Throughout this discussion, we restrict attention to systems which always select the leftmost atom in a goal. Cut is simply a non-logical annotation of programs which conveys certain control information to the system. Although it is written like an atom in the body of a clause, it is not an atom and has no logical significance at all. On the other hand, for pedagogical reasons, it is sometimes convenient to regard it as an atom which succeeds immediately on being called. The declarative semantics of a program with cuts is exactly the declarative semantics of the program with the cuts removed. In other words, the cuts do not in any way modify the declarative reading of the program.

What, then, is the nature of the control information conveyed by a cut? First, we need some terminology. Let us call the goal which caused the clause containing the cut to be activated, the *parent* goal. That is, the selected atom in the parent matched the head of the clause whose body contains the cut. Now, when "selected", the cut simply "succeeds" immediately. However, if backtracking later returns to the cut, the system discontinues searching in the subtree which has the parent goal at the root. The cut thus causes the remainder of that subtree to be pruned from the SLD-tree.

To clarify this, consider the following program fragment

A ← B, C
.
.
B ← D, !, E
.
.
D ←
.
.

where A, B, C, D and E are atoms. In Figure 5, we show part of the SLD-tree for a call to this program. The selected atom B in the goal ←B,C causes the cut to be introduced. The atom D is then selected and succeeds. The cut then succeeds, but the subgoal E eventually fails and the system backtracks to the cut. At this point, "deep" backtracking occurs. The system discontinues any

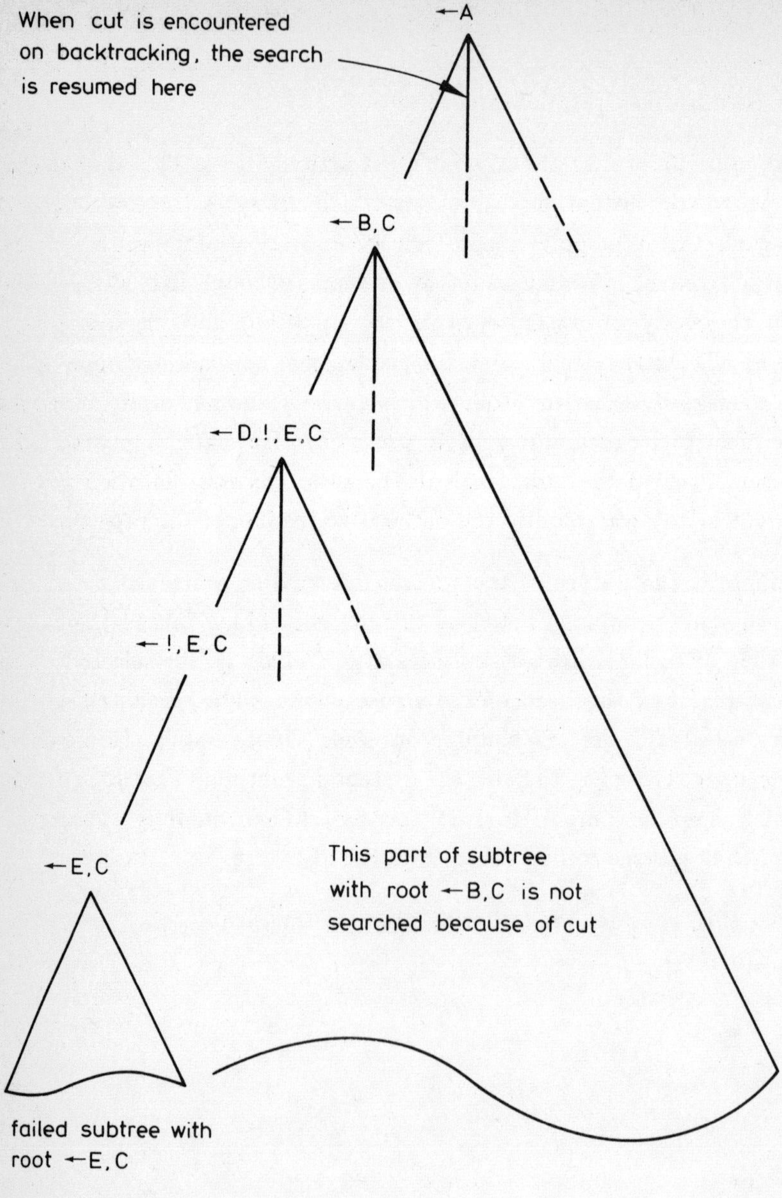

Fig. 5. The effect of cut

resumes the search with the next choice for the goal ←A. This can be implemented very simply by popping goals from the goal stack until the goal ←A becomes top of the stack.

So a cut "merely" prunes the SLD-tree. Is it possible that a cut can somehow be harmful? The key issue is whether or not there is an answer to the (top level) goal in the part of the SLD-tree thus pruned by the cut. If there is no answer in the pruned part (that is, if the pruned part does not contain a success branch), then we call such a use of cut *safe*. However, if a success branch gets pruned by the cut, we call such a use of cut *unsafe*. Safe uses of cut are beneficial – they improve efficiency without missing answers. Unsafe uses of cut are harmful to the extent that a correct answer substitution is missed.

Thus the harmful effect of cuts is that they can introduce a form of incompleteness into the SLD-resolution implementation of correct answer substitution. Theorem 9.5 assures us that every correct answer substitution can be computed. However, a cut in a program can destroy the completeness guaranteed by this theorem.

Note that this form of incompleteness is of a different nature to the form of incompleteness mentioned in §10, which occurs because a depth-first search can get lost down an infinite branch. A system which allows the search to become lost down an infinite branch does not give any answer at all (only a stack overflow message!). With an unsafe use of cut, a system can answer "no" when it should have answered "yes". However you look at it, the system has given an incorrect answer.

But, there is a further, much more harmful, effect of cuts. This occurs when programmers take advantage of cuts to write programs which are not even declaratively correct. For example, consider the program

max(x,y,y) ← x≤y, !
max(x,y,x) ←

where max(x,y,z) is intended to be true iff z is the maximum of x and y. Advantage has been taken of the effect of the cut to leave the test x>y out of the second clause. Procedurally, the semantics of the above program is the maximum relation. Declaratively, it is something else entirely. Such programs programming.

Admittedly, there are occasions when efficiency considerations force the use of such aberrations. However, it is far better for programmers, whenever possible, to make use of such higher level facilities as (sound implementations of) if-then-else, negation and not equals, which are not only reasonably efficient, but also lead to programs whose declarative semantics more accurately reflects the relation being computed.

PROBLEMS FOR CHAPTER 2

1. Give an example of a correct answer substitution, which is not R-computed, for any computation rule R.

2. Let P be the slowsort program, G be the goal ←sort(1.0.nil,y) and R be the computation rule which always selects the leftmost atom. Show directly that P ∪ {G} has an SLD-refutation via R.

3. Consider the program

   leaves(tree(void,v,void),v.x–x) ←

   leaves(tree(u,v,w),x–y) ← leaves(u,x–z), leaves(w,z–y)

Find a goal such that a PROLOG system without the occur check will answer the goal incorrectly.

4. Find an example to show that $A \in T_P \uparrow n$, for some $n \in \omega$, does not necessarily imply that there exists an SLD-refutation of *length* $\leq n$ for P ∪ {←A}.

5. Let P be a program and A an atom. Prove or disprove the following: ∀(A) is a logical consequence of P iff $[A] \subseteq T_P \uparrow n$, for some $n \in \omega$.

6. Complete the details of the proof of theorem 9.2.

7. Let P be the program

   p(x) ← q(x), r(x)

   q(a) ←

   r(x) ← r_1(x)

$r_1(a) \leftarrow$

Let R be the computation rule which always selects the leftmost atom and R′ be the computation rule which always selects the rightmost atom. Use the switching lemma to transform the refutation of P ∪ {←p(x)} via R into one via R′.

8. Complete the details of the proof of theorem 10.3.

9. Let P be the program

p(a,b) ←
p(c,b) ←
p(x,z) ← p(x,y), p(y,z)
p(x,y) ← p(y,x)

and G be the goal ←p(a,c). Show that, if any clause of P is omitted, P ∪ {G} does not have a refutation (no matter what the computation rule).

10. Find a program P and a goal G such that each SLD-tree for P ∪ {G} has two success branches, but no depth-first search will ever find *both* success branches no matter what the computation rule and even if the program clauses can be dynamically reordered for each call to each definition of the program.

11. Let P be the slowsort program and G be the goal ←sort(1.0.2.nil,y). Find an SLD-refutation of P ∪ {G} using a computation rule which suitably delays calls to sorted.

12. What problems arise in a PROLOG system which allows coroutining computation rules and also has the cut facility? How might these problems be solved?

Chapter 3. NEGATION

In this chapter, we study various forms of negation. Since only positive information can be a logical consequence of a program, special rules are needed to deduce negative information. The most important of these rules are the closed world assumption and the negation as failure rule. The major results of this chapter are the soundness and completeness of the negation as failure rule.

§12. NEGATIVE INFORMATION

Logic programs have a database interpretation, which generalizes the concept of a relational database. The ground unit clauses of a program are specific facts. They can be thought of as the individual tuples in relations. However, programs generalize relational databases because they allow the definition of rules, that is, non-ground program clauses (usually conditional). The use of rules, in what are called *deductive databases* [37], has important consequences, which are explored much more fully in [20] and [21]. Briefly, the answering of a query on a deductive database becomes more of a computation, rather than simply a retrieval of information. Moreover, logic is used as a uniform language for data, programs, views, queries and integrity constraints.

Of course, deductive databases are different from logic programs in that databases generally have a very large number of facts, but only a few rules, while logic programs generally have more rules than facts. This difference is inessential. From a theoretical point of view, a database is just a logic program. Traditionally, negation has been discussed from the database viewpoint. While we will occasionally refer to this context, most of the discussion and all the results will be stated in the context of logic programs.

The inference system we have studied so far is very specialized. SLD-resolution applies only to sets of Horn clauses with exactly one goal clause. Using SLD-resolution, we can never deduce negative information. To be precise, let P be a program and $A \in B_P$. Then we cannot prove that $\sim A$ is a logical consequence of P. The reason is that $P \cup \{A\}$ is satisfiable, having B_P as a model.

To illustrate this, consider the program

student(joe) ←

student(bill) ←

student(jim) ←

teacher(mary) ←

Now suppose we wish to establish that mary is not a student, that is, ~student(mary). As we have shown above, ~student(mary) is not a logical consequence of the program. However, note that student(mary) is also not a logical consequence of the program. What we can do now is invoke a special inference rule: if a ground atom A is not a logical consequence of a program, then infer ~A. This inference rule is called the *closed world assumption* (CWA). (Because of the approach taken here to the CWA, we would have preferred it to have been called the closed world *rule*. For additional discussion of the CWA, see [20]). Under this inference rule, we are entitled to infer ~student(mary) on the grounds that student(mary) is not a logical consequence of the program.

The CWA is often a very natural rule to use in a database context. In relational databases, this rule is generally applied - information not explicitly present in the database is taken to be false. Of course, in deductive databases, the situation is complicated by the presence of rules in the database. The information content of the database is not determined by mere inspection. It is now the set of all things which can be deduced from the database. Whether or not use of the CWA is justified must be determined for each particular database application. While it is generally natural to use the CWA, its use may not always be justified. The contrary assumption, that the CWA can not be used, is called the *open world assumption*.

The CWA is an example of a non-monotonic inference rule. Such rules are currently of great interest in artificial intelligence [6]. An inference rule is that previously held. As an example, if we add sufficient facts and rules to the above program so as to be able to deduce student(mary), then we will no longer be able to use the CWA to infer ~student(mary).

Now let us consider a program P for which the CWA is applicable. Let $A \in B_P$ and suppose we wish to infer ~A. In order to use the CWA, we have to show that A is not a logical consequence of P. Unfortunately, because of the undecidability of first order logic, there is no algorithm which will take an arbitrary A as input and respond in a finite amount of time with the answer whether A is or is not a logical consequence of P. If A is not a logical consequence, it may loop forever. Thus, in practice, the application of the CWA is generally restricted to those $A \in B_P$ whose attempted proofs fail finitely. Let us make this idea precise.

Definition Let P be a program and G a goal. A *finitely failed* SLD-tree for $P \cup \{G\}$ is one which is finite and contains no success branches.

Definition Let P be a program. The *SLD finite failure set* of P is the set of all $A \in B_P$ for which there exists a finitely failed SLD-tree for $P \cup \{\leftarrow A\}$.

Note carefully in this last definition that there is no requirement that all SLD-trees fail finitely, only that there exists at least one. It follows from earlier results that if A is in the SLD finite failure set of P, then A is not a logical consequence of P and every SLD-tree for $P \cup \{\leftarrow A\}$ contains only infinite or failure branches.

Now let us return to the CWA. In order to show that $A \in B_P$ is not a logical consequence of P, we can try giving ←A as a goal to the system. Let us assume that A is not, in fact, in the success set of P. Now there are two possibilities: either A is in the SLD finite failure set or it is not. If A is in the SLD finite failure set, then the system can construct a finitely failed SLD-tree and return the answer "no". The CWA then allows us to infer ~A. In the other case, each SLD-tree has at least one infinite branch. Thus, unless the system has a mechanism for detecting infinite branches, it will never be able to complete the task of showing that A is not a logical consequence of P.

These considerations lead us to another non-monotonic inference rule, called the *negation as failure rule* [10], which is also used to infer negative information. This rule states that if A is in the SLD finite failure set of P, then infer ~A. Since the SLD finite failure set is a subset of the complement of the success set, we see that the negation as failure rule is less powerful than the CWA. However, in practice, implementing anything beyond negation as failure is difficult. The possibility of extending negation as failure closer to the CWA by adding mechanisms for detecting infinite branches has hardly been explored.

Negation as failure is easily and efficiently implemented by "reversing" the notions of success and failure. Suppose $A \in B_P$ and we have the goal ← ~A. The system tries the goal ←A. If ←A succeeds, then ← ~A fails, while if it fails finitely, then ← ~A succeeds.

Programs only contain the if halves of the definitions of their predicates. This is the reason that only positive information can be deduced. In order to deduce negative information, we could add the only-if halves of the definitions. In our previous example, if we add the missing only-if half to the definition of student, we obtain

$$\forall x\ (\mathrm{student}(x) \leftrightarrow (x=\mathrm{joe}) \vee (x=\mathrm{bill}) \vee (x=\mathrm{jim}))$$

Adding appropriate axioms for =, we can now deduce ~student(mary). This process of adding the only-if halves of the definitions of the various predicates is called "completing" the program. We shall study the completion in §14. Its relationship to the CWA and the negation as failure rule will be made precise in §14 and §15.

§13. FINITE FAILURE

The main results of this section are several characterizations of the finite failure set of a program.

First, we must give the definition of the finite failure set of a program. The usual definition of finite failure ([2], [10]) is what we called SLD finite failure in the previous section. In fact, this is actually the *implementation* of the declarative concept of finite failure, the definition of which was first given by Lassez and Maher [34].

Definition Let P be a program. Then F_P^d, the set of atoms in B_P which are *finitely failed by depth d*, is defined as follows:

(b) $A \in F_P^d$, for $d>1$, if for each clause $B \leftarrow B_1,\ldots,B_n$ in P and each substitution θ such that $A=B\theta$ and $B_1\theta,\ldots,B_n\theta$ are ground, there exists k such that $1 \leq k \leq n$ and $B_k\theta \in F_P^{d-1}$.

Definition The *finite failure set* F_P of P is defined by $F_P = \cup_{d \geq 1} F_P^d$.

Note the following simple relationship between F_P and $T_P \downarrow \omega$ (see problem 1).

Proposition 13.1 Let P be a program. Then $F_P = B_P \backslash T_P \downarrow \omega$.

Our main task is to establish the equivalence of F_P and the SLD finite failure set. We begin with two lemmas, due to Apt and van Emden [2], whose easy proofs are omitted.

Lemma 13.2 Let P be a program, G a goal and θ a substitution. Suppose that $P \cup \{G\}$ has a finitely failed SLD-tree of depth $\leq$ k. Then $P \cup \{G\theta\}$ also has a finitely failed SLD-tree of depth $\leq$ k.

Lemma 13.3 Let P be a program and $A_i \in B_P$, for $i=1,\ldots,m$. Suppose that $P \cup \{\leftarrow A_1,\ldots,A_m\}$ has a finitely failed SLD-tree of depth $\leq$ k. Then there exists $i \in \{1,\ldots,m\}$ such that $P \cup \{\leftarrow A_i\}$ has a finitely failed SLD-tree of depth $\leq$ k.

The next proposition is due to Apt and van Emden [2].

Proposition 13.4 Let P be a program and $A \in B_P$. If $P \cup \{\leftarrow A\}$ has a finitely failed SLD-tree of depth $\leq$ k, then $A \notin T_P \downarrow k$.

Proof Suppose first that $P \cup \{\leftarrow A\}$ has a finitely failed SLD-tree of depth 1. Then $A \notin T_P \downarrow 1$.

Now assume the result holds for k-1. Suppose that $P \cup \{\leftarrow A\}$ has a finitely failed SLD-tree of depth $\leq$ k. Suppose, to obtain a contradiction, that $A \in T_P \downarrow k$. Then there exists a clause $B \leftarrow B_1,\ldots,B_n$ in P such that $A=B\theta$ and $\{B_1\theta,\ldots,B_n\theta\} \subseteq T_P \downarrow (k-1)$, for some ground substitution θ. Thus there exists an mgu γ such that $A\gamma=B\gamma$ and $\theta=\gamma\sigma$, for some σ. Now $\leftarrow(B_1,\ldots,B_n)\gamma$ is the root of a finitely failed SLD-tree of depth $\leq$ k-1. By lemma 13.2, so also is $\leftarrow(B_1,\ldots,B_n)\theta$. Lemma 13.3 now gives that some $\leftarrow B_i\theta$ is the root of a finitely failed SLD-tree of depth $\leq$ k-1. By the induction hypothesis, $B_i\theta \notin T_P \downarrow (k-1)$, which gives the contradiction ∎

It is interesting that the (strict) converse of proposition 13.4 does not hold (see problem 4). Next we note that SLD finite failure only guarantees the existence of one finitely failed SLD-tree - others may be infinite. It would be helpful to identify exactly those computation rules which guarantee to find a finitely failed SLD-tree, if one exists at all. The definition of such a class was given by Lassez and Maher [34].

Definition An SLD-derivation is *fair* if it is either failed or, for every atom B in the derivation, (some further instantiated version of) B is selected within a finite number of steps.

Definition A computation rule is *fair* if every SLD-derivation using the rule is fair.

Note that the standard PROLOG computation rule is not fair.

Proposition 13.5 Let P be a program and $\leftarrow A_1,...,A_m$ be a goal. Suppose there is a non-failed fair derivation $\leftarrow A_1,...,A_m=G_0, G_1,...$ with mgu's $\theta_1, \theta_2,...$. Then, given $k\in\omega$, there exists $n\in\omega$ such that $[A_i\theta_1...\theta_n] \subseteq T_P\downarrow k$, for $i=1,...,m$.

Proof Theorem 7.4 shows that we can assume that the derivation is infinite. Clearly it suffices to show that given $i\in\{1,...,m\}$ and $k\in\omega$, there exists $n\in\omega$ such that $[A_i\theta_1...\theta_n] \subseteq T_P\downarrow k$.

Fix $i\in\{1,...,m\}$. The result is clearly true for $k=0$. Assume it is true for $k-1$. Suppose $A_i\theta_1...\theta_{p-1}$ is selected in the goal G_{p-1}. (By fairness, A_i must eventually be selected). Let G_p be $\leftarrow B_1,...,B_q$, where $q\geq 1$. By the induction hypothesis, there exists $s\in\omega$ such that $\cup_{j=1}^{q}[B_j\theta_{p+1}...\theta_{p+s}] \subseteq T_P\downarrow(k-1)$. Hence we have that $[A_i\theta_1...\theta_{p+s}] \subseteq T_P(\cup_{j=1}^{q}[B_j\theta_{p+1}...\theta_{p+s}]) \subseteq T_P(T_P\downarrow(k-1)) = T_P\downarrow k$ ∎

Combining the results of Apt and van Emden [2] and Lassez and Maher [34], we can now obtain the characterizations of the finite failure set.

Theorem 13.6 Let P be a program and $A\in B_P$. Then the following are equivalent:

(a) $A\in F_P$.

(b) $A\notin T_P\downarrow\omega$.

(c) A is in the SLD finite failure set.

(d) For every fair computation rule R, the corresponding SLD-tree for $P \cup \{\leftarrow A\}$ via R is finitely failed.

Proof (a) is equivalent to (b) by proposition 13.1. That (d) implies (c) is obvious. Also (c) implies (b) by proposition 13.4.

Finally, suppose that (d) does not hold. Hence there exists a non-failed fair derivation for $\leftarrow A$. Proposition 13.5 then shows that $A \in T_P \downarrow \omega$ and thus (b) does not hold ∎

Theorem 13.6 shows that fair SLD-resolution is a sound and complete implementation of finite failure.

§14. PROGRAMMING WITH THE COMPLETION

In this section, general programs are introduced. These are programs whose program clauses may contain negative literals in their body. The completion of a general program is also defined. The completion will play an important part in the soundness and completeness results for the negation as failure rule. The definition of a correct answer substitution is extended to the completion of a general program.

Logic programs, as considered so far, lack sufficient expressiveness for many situations. The problem is that often a negative condition is needed in the body of a clause. As an example, consider the clause

$p(x,y) \leftarrow \sim q(x), r(y)$

whose declarative reading is that, for all x and y, p(x,y) is true if q(x) is false and r(y) is true. Practical PROLOG programs often require such extra expressiveness. Thus it is important to extend the definition of programs to include negative literals in the bodies of clauses. Of course, logic programming systems also require a mechanism for handling such negative subgoals. The method usually chosen is to augment SLD-resolution with the negation as failure rule. This is examined in detail in §15 and §16.

Definition A *general program clause* is a clause of the form

$$A \leftarrow L_1,\ldots,L_n$$

where A is an atom and $L_1,\ldots,L_n$ are literals.

Definition A *general program* is a finite set of general program clauses.

Definition A *general goal* is a clause of the form

$$\leftarrow L_1,\ldots,L_n$$

where $L_1,\ldots,L_n$ are literals.

Every program is a general program, but not conversely. It is easy to see that the definition of T_P can be extended naturally to general programs. However, it is important to appreciate that T_P is not nearly so useful in this more general setting because it is no longer monotonic. Thus the fixpoint results developed in §5 are not applicable.

In order to justify the use of the negation as failure rule, Clark [10] introduced the idea of the completion of a general program. We next give the definition of the completion.

Let $p(t_1,\ldots,t_n)\leftarrow L_1,\ldots,L_m$ be a general program clause in a general program P. We will require a new predicate $=$, not appearing in P, whose intended interpretation is the identity relation. The first step is to transform the given clause into

$$p(x_1,\ldots,x_n)\leftarrow(x_1=t_1)\wedge\ldots\wedge(x_n=t_n)\wedge L_1\wedge\ldots\wedge L_m$$

where $x_1,\ldots,x_n$ are variables not appearing in the clause. Then, if $y_1,\ldots,y_d$ are the variables of the original clause, we transform this into

$$p(x_1,\ldots,x_n)\leftarrow\exists y_1\ldots\exists y_d\ ((x_1=t_1)\wedge\ldots\wedge(x_n=t_n)\wedge L_1\wedge\ldots\wedge L_m)$$

Now suppose this transformation is made for each clause in the definition of p. Then we obtain $k\geq 1$ transformed clauses of the form

$$p(x_1,\ldots,x_n)\leftarrow E_1$$

$$\vdots$$

$$p(x_1,\ldots,x_n)\leftarrow E_k$$

where each E_i has the general form

$$\exists y_1\ldots\exists y_d\ ((x_1=t_1)\wedge\ldots\wedge(x_n=t_n)\wedge L_1\wedge\ldots\wedge L_m)$$

The *completed definition* of p is then the formula

$$\forall x_1\ldots\forall x_n\ (p(x_1,\ldots,x_n)\leftrightarrow E_1\vee\ldots\vee E_k)$$

Example Let the definition of a predicate p be

$p(y) \leftarrow q(y), \sim r(a,y)$

$p(f(z)) \leftarrow \sim q(z)$

$p(b) \leftarrow$

Then the completed definition of p is

$$\forall x\ (p(x) \longleftrightarrow (\exists y\ ((x=y) \wedge q(y) \wedge \sim r(a,y)) \vee \exists z\ ((x=f(z)) \wedge \sim q(z)) \vee (x=b)))$$

Example The completed definition of the predicate student from the example in §12 is

$$\forall x\ (student(x) \longleftrightarrow (x=joe) \vee (x=bill) \vee (x=jim))$$

Some predicates in the general program may very well not appear in the head of any general program clause. For each such predicate q, we explicitly add the clause

$$\forall x_1 ... \forall x_n\ \sim q(x_1,...,x_n)$$

This is the definition of such q given implicitly by the general program. We also call this clause the *completed definition* of such q.

It is essential to also include some axioms which constrain =. The following *equality theory* is sufficient for our purpose. In these axioms, we use the standard notation $\neq$ for not equals.

1. $c \neq d$, for all pairs c,d of distinct constants.
2. $\forall (f(x_1,...,x_n) \neq g(y_1,...,y_m))$, for all pairs f,g of distinct functions.
3. $\forall (f(x_1,...,x_n) \neq c)$, for each constant c and function f.
4. $\forall (t[x] \neq x)$, for each non-variable term t[x] containing x.
5. $\forall ((x_1 \neq y_1) \vee ... \vee (x_n \neq y_n) \rightarrow f(x_1,...,x_n) \neq f(y_1,...,y_n))$, for each function f.
6. $\forall (x=x)$.
7. $\forall ((x_1=y_1) \wedge ... \wedge (x_n=y_n) \rightarrow f(x_1,...,x_n)=f(y_1,...,y_n))$, for each function f.
8. $\forall ((x_1=y_1) \wedge ... \wedge (x_n=y_n) \rightarrow (p(x_1,...,x_n) \rightarrow p(y_1,...,y_n)))$, for each predicate p (including =).

Definition Let P be a general program. The *completion* of P, denoted comp(P), is the collection of completed definitions for each predicate in P together with the equality theory.

Axioms 6, 7 and 8 are the usual axioms for first order theories with equality. Note that axioms 6 and 8 together imply that = is an equivalence relation. The equality theory places a strong restriction on the possible interpretations of =. This restriction is essential to obtain the desired justification of negation as failure. Roughly speaking, we are forcing = to be interpreted as the identity relation on U_P (see problem 10).

Now, as Clark [10] has pointed out, it is best to regard the *completion* of the general program, not the general program itself, as the prime object of interest. Even though a programmer only gives a logic programming system the general program, the understanding is that, conceptually, the general program is completed by the system and that the programmer is actually programming with the completion. Corresponding to this notion, we have the concept of a correct answer substitution. The problem then arises of showing that SLD-resolution, augmented with the negation as failure rule, is a sound and complete implementation of the declarative concept of a correct answer substitution. We tackle this problem in §15 and §16.

Definition Let P be a general program and G a general goal $\leftarrow L_1,\ldots,L_n$. A *correct answer substitution* for comp(P) $\cup$ {G} is an answer substitution θ such that $\forall((L_1 \wedge \ldots \wedge L_n)\theta)$ is a logical consequence of comp(P).

It is important to establish that this definition generalizes the definition of correct answer substitution given in §4. The first result we need to prove this is the following proposition.

Proposition 14.1 Let P be a general program. Then P is a logical consequence of comp(P).

Proof Let M be a model for comp(P). We have to show that M is a model for P. Let $p(t_1,\ldots,t_n) \leftarrow L_1,\ldots,L_m$ be a general clause in P and suppose that $L_1,\ldots,L_m$ are true in M, for some assignment of the variables $y_1,\ldots,y_d$ in the clause.

Consider the completed definition of p

$$\forall x_1 \ldots \forall x_n \ (p(x_1,\ldots,x_n) \leftrightarrow E_1 \vee \ldots \vee E_k)$$

and suppose E_i is

$$\exists y_1 \ldots \exists y_d \ ((x_1 = t_1) \wedge \ldots \wedge (x_n = t_n) \wedge L_1 \wedge \ldots \wedge L_m)$$

Now let x_j be t_j $(1 \leq j \leq n)$, for the same assignment of the variables $y_1,\ldots,y_d$ as above. Thus E_i is true in M, since $L_1,\ldots,L_m$ are true in M and also since M must satisfy axiom 6. Hence $p(t_1,\ldots,t_n)$ is true in M ∎

The next task is to generalize the mapping T_P.

Definition A *pre-interpretation* of a first order language L consists of the following:

(a) A non-empty set D, called the *domain* of the pre-interpretation.

(b) For each constant in L, the assignment of an element in D.

Definition Let J be a pre-interpretation of a first order language L. An interpretation I of L is *based on* J if I has the same domain and assignment of constants and functions as J.

Corresponding to a fixed pre-interpretation J, there will in general be numerous interpretations based on J obtained by further specifying the assignment of the predicates of L. In fact, as for Herbrand interpretations, each interpretation based on J can be identified with some subset of "atoms" (where the predicate of each "atom" is in L and each argument is in D). We simply make $p(d_1,...,d_n)$ true precisely when $p(d_1,...,d_n)$ is in this subset. Furthermore, the set of all interpretations based on a pre-interpretation J is a complete lattice under the partial order of set inclusion.

As before, we will find it convenient to refer to a pre-interpretation of a program rather than the underlying first order language.

Definition Let J be a pre-interpretation of a program P. We define a mapping, denoted by T_P^J, from the lattice of interpretations based on J to itself as follows. Let I be an interpretation based on J. Then $T_P^J(I) = \{p(d_1,...,d_n) : B \leftarrow B_1,...,B_n$ is an "instance" of a clause in P using the assignments given by J and some assignment of variables such that B is $p(d_1,...,d_n)$ and $\{B_1,...,B_n\} \subseteq I\}$.

Clearly T_P^J is monotonic. T_P is the special case of T_P^J obtained by taking J to be the pre-interpretation of P with domain U_P and assignment of constants and functions as for Herbrand interpretations. Many of the properties of T_P extend easily to T_P^J. For example, the following proposition generalizes proposition 6.4.

Proposition 14.2 Let P be a program, J a pre-interpretation of P and I an interpretation based on J. Then I is a model for P iff $T_P^J(I) \subseteq I$.

The next result shows that fixpoints of T_P^J give models for comp(P).

Proposition 14.3 Let P be a program and J a pre-interpretation of P. Let I be an interpretation based on J and suppose that I, together with = assigned the identity relation, is a model for the equality theory. Then I is a fixpoint of T_P^J iff I, together with = assigned the identity relation, is a model for comp(P).

Proof Suppose first that $I=T_P^J(I)$. Since we have assumed that I, together with = assigned the identity relation, is a model for the equality theory, it suffices to show that this interpretation is a model for each of the completed definitions of comp(P). Consider a completed definition of the form $\forall x_1 \ldots \forall x_n \sim q(x_1,\ldots,x_n)$. Since I is a fixpoint, it is clear that the interpretation is a model of this formula. Now consider a completed definition of the form

$$\forall x_1 \ldots \forall x_n\ (p(x_1,\ldots,x_n) \leftrightarrow E_1 \vee \ldots \vee E_k)$$

Since $T_P^J(I) \subseteq I$, it follows that the interpretation is a model for the formula

$$\forall x_1 \ldots \forall x_n\ (p(x_1,\ldots,x_n) \leftarrow E_1 \vee \ldots \vee E_k)$$

Similarly, since $T_P^J(I) \supseteq I$, it follows that the interpretation is a model for the formula

$$\forall x_1 \ldots \forall x_n\ (p(x_1,\ldots,x_n) \rightarrow E_1 \vee \ldots \vee E_k)$$

Conversely, suppose that I, together with = assigned the identity relation, is a model for the completion. Then using the fact that the interpretation is a model for formulas of the form

$$\forall x_1 \ldots \forall x_n\ (p(x_1,\ldots,x_n) \leftarrow E_1 \vee \ldots \vee E_k)$$

it follows that $T_P^J(I) \subseteq I$. Similarly, using the fact that the interpretation is a model for formulas of the form

$$\forall x_1 \ldots \forall x_n\ (p(x_1,\ldots,x_n) \rightarrow E_1 \vee \ldots \vee E_k)$$

it follows that $T_P^J(I) \supseteq I$ ∎

Proposition 14.4 Let P be a program and $A_1,\ldots,A_m$ be atoms. If $\forall(A_1 \wedge \ldots \wedge A_m)$ is a logical consequence of comp(P), then it is also a logical consequence of P.

Proof Let $x_1,\ldots,x_k$ be the variables in $A_1 \wedge \ldots \wedge A_m$. We have to show that $\forall x_1 \ldots \forall x_k\ (A_1 \wedge \ldots \wedge A_m)$ is a logical consequence of P, that is, $P \cup \{\sim\forall x_1 \ldots \forall x_k\ (A_1 \wedge \ldots \wedge A_m)\}$ is unsatisfiable or, equivalently, $S = P \cup \{\sim A_1' \vee \ldots \vee \sim A_m'\}$ is unsatisfiable, where A_i' is A_i with $x_1,\ldots,x_k$ replaced by appropriate Skolem constants.

Since S is in clause form, we can restrict attention to Herbrand interpretations of S. Let I be a Herbrand interpretation of S. We can also regard I as an interpretation of P. (Note that I is not necessarily a Herbrand interpretation of P). Suppose I is a model for P. Consider the pre-interpretation J obtained from I by ignoring the assignment of the predicates in I. By proposition 14.2, we have that $T_P^J(I) \subseteq I$. Since T_P^J is monotonic, proposition 5.2 shows that there exists a fixpoint $I' \subseteq I$ of T_P^J. Since I′

together with = assigned the identity relation, is obviously a model for the equality theory, proposition 14.3 shows that this interpretation is a model for comp(P). Hence $\sim A_1' \vee ... \vee \sim A_m'$ is false in this interpretation. Since $I' \subseteq I$, we have that $\sim A_1' \vee ... \vee \sim A_m'$ is false in I. Thus S is unsatisfiable ∎

Note that by combining propositions 14.1 and 14.4, it follows that the *positive* information which can be deduced from comp(P) is exactly the same as the positive information which can be deduced from P. To be precise, we have the following result.

Theorem 14.5 Let P be a program and G a goal. Let θ be an answer substitution. Then θ is a correct answer substitution for comp(P) $\cup$ {G} iff θ is a correct answer substitution for P $\cup$ {G}.

Theorem 14.5 shows that the definition of correct answer substitution given in this section generalizes the definition given in §4.

Finally, we record two results for later use.

Proposition 14.6 Let P be a program and I a Herbrand interpretation of P. Then $I \cup \{s=s : s \in U_P\}$ is a model for comp(P) iff $I = T_P(I)$.

Proof It is clear that $I \cup \{s=s : s \in U_P\}$ is a model for the equality theory. Hence the result follows from proposition 14.3 ∎

Proposition 14.7 Let P be a program and $A \in B_P$. Then $A \notin gfp(T_P)$ iff comp(P) $\cup$ {A} has no Herbrand model.

Proof Suppose $A \in gfp(T_P)$. Then $gfp(T_P) \cup \{s=s : s \in U_P\}$ is a Herbrand model for comp(P) $\cup$ {A}, by proposition 14.6.

Conversely, suppose comp(P) $\cup$ {A} has a Herbrand model M. By the equality theory, = must be assigned the identity relation on U_P in the model M. Thus M has the form $I \cup \{s=s : s \in U_P\}$, for some Herbrand interpretation I of P. Hence $I = T_P(I)$, by proposition 14.6, and so $A \in gfp(T_P)$ ∎

§15. SOUNDNESS OF THE NEGATION AS FAILURE RULE

In section §14, we introduced the fundamental concept of a correct answer substitution for comp(P) $\cup$ {G}. Now that we have the appropriate declarative concept, let us see how we can implement it. The basic idea is to use SLD-resolution, augmented with the negation as failure rule (SLDNF-resolution). In this section, we prove the soundness of the negation as failure rule and SLDNF-resolution.

Before giving the definition of SLDNF-resolution, we first specify an appropriate class of computation rules.

Definition A computation rule R (for SLDNF-resolution) is *safe* if the following conditions are satisfied:
(a) R only selects negative literals which are ground.
(b) Having selected a ground negative literal ~A in some goal, R attempts to finish the construction of a finitely failed SLDNF-tree with root ←A before continuing with the remainder of the computation.

There are no restrictions at all on the selection of positive literals. We can regard the negative literal subgoals as separate *lemmas*, which must be established in order to compute the result. The goal answering process is entered recursively to establish these lemmas.

The restriction that R selects only *ground* negative literals is the usual one. We discuss the possibility of lifting this restriction later.

Definition Let P be a general program, G be a general goal and R be a safe computation rule. An *SLDNF-derivation* G_0=G, G_1,... of P ∪ {G} via R is defined as follows:
(a) Suppose G_i is $\leftarrow L_1,\ldots,L_k$ and R selects the positive literal L_m. Suppose $A \leftarrow M_1,\ldots,M_q$ is the input clause and L_m and A have mgu θ_{i+1}. Then the derived general goal G_{i+1} is

$$\leftarrow (L_1,\ldots,L_{m-1},M_1,\ldots,M_q,L_{m+1},\ldots,L_k)\theta_{i+1}$$

(b) Suppose G_i is $\leftarrow L_1,\ldots,L_k$ and R selects the ground negative literal L_m, where L_m is ~A. An attempt is made to construct a finitely failed SLDNF-tree with ←A at the root. If the goal ←A succeeds, then the subgoal ~A fails and so the goal G_i also fails. If ←A fails finitely, then the subgoal ~A succeeds and the derived general goal G_{i+1} is

$$\leftarrow L_1,\ldots,L_{m-1},L_{m+1},\ldots,L_k$$

In the latter case, θ_{i+1} is the identity substitution.

of theorem 15.3 that $\leftarrow(L_1,\ldots,L_{m-1},M_1,\ldots,M_q,L_{m+1},\ldots,L_k)\theta_{i+1}$ is clearly a logical consequence of $\leftarrow L_1,\ldots,L_k$ and $A\leftarrow M_1,\ldots,M_q$.

Note that bindings are only made by successful calls of positive literals. Negative literal calls never create bindings; they only succeed or fail. Thus negation as failure is purely a test. As such, it is a rather unsatisfactory replacement for (logical) negation.

Definition Let P be a general program, G a general goal and R a safe computation rule. An *SLDNF-refutation* of $P \cup \{G\}$ via R is an SLDNF-derivation which ends in the empty clause.

Definition Let P be a general program, G a general goal and R a safe computation rule. Then the *SLDNF-tree* for $P \cup \{G\}$ via R is defined as follows:
(a) Each node of the tree is a general goal.
(b) The root node is G.
(c) Let $\leftarrow L_1,\ldots,L_k$ $(k\geq 1)$ be a node in the tree and suppose that the literal selected by R is the positive literal L_m. Then this node has a descendent for each input clause $A\leftarrow M_1,\ldots,M_q$ such that L_m and A are unifiable. The descendent is

$$\leftarrow(L_1,\ldots,L_{m-1},M_1,\ldots,M_q,L_{m+1},\ldots,L_k)\theta$$

where θ is an mgu of L_m and A.
(d) Let $\leftarrow L_1,\ldots,L_k$ $(k\geq 1)$ be a node in the tree and suppose that the literal selected by R is the ground negative literal L_m. If the subgoal L_m is successful, then the single descendent of the node is

$$\leftarrow L_1,\ldots,L_{m-1},L_{m+1},\ldots,L_k$$

If the subgoal L_m fails, then the node has no descendents.
(e) Nodes which are the empty clause have no descendents.

The concepts of SLDNF-derivation, SLDNF-refutation and SLDNF-tree generalize those of SLD-derivation, SLD-refutation and SLD-tree.

Definition Let P be a general program, G a general goal and R a safe computation rule. An *R-computed answer substitution* θ for $P \cup \{G\}$ is the substitution obtained by restricting the composition $\theta_1\ldots\theta_n$ to the variables of G, where $\theta_1,\ldots,\theta_n$ is the sequence of mgu's used in an SLDNF-refutation of $P \cup \{G\}$ via R.

Since R only selects negative literals which are ground, it follows that $L_i\theta$ must be ground, for each negative literal L_i in G. This definition extends the definition of an R-computed answer substitution given in §7.

The first major result of this section is the soundness of the negation as failure rule. In preparation for the proof of this result, we establish two lemmas due to Clark [10].

Lemma 15.1 Let $p(s_1,...,s_n)$ and $p(t_1,...,t_n)$ be atoms.
(a) If $p(s_1,...,s_n)$ and $p(t_1,...,t_n)$ are not unifiable, then $\sim\exists((s_1=t_1)\wedge...\wedge(s_n=t_n))$ is a logical consequence of the equality theory.
(b) If $p(s_1,...,s_n)$ and $p(t_1,...,t_n)$ are unifiable with mgu $\theta = \{x_1/r_1, ...,x_k/r_k\}$, then $\forall((s_1=t_1)\wedge...\wedge(s_n=t_n)\leftrightarrow(x_1=r_1)\wedge...\wedge(x_k=r_k))$ is a logical consequence of the equality theory.

Proof Suppose that $p(s_1,...,s_n)$ and $p(t_1,...,t_n)$ are unifiable with mgu $\theta = \{x_1/r_1,...,x_k/r_k\}$. Then it follows from equality axioms 6, 7 and 8 that $\forall((s_1=t_1)\wedge...\wedge(s_n=t_n)\leftarrow(x_1=r_1)\wedge...\wedge(x_k=r_k))$ is a logical consequence of the equality theory. The remainder of the lemma is proved by induction on the number of steps k of an attempt by the unification algorithm to unify $p(s_1,...,s_n)$ and $p(t_1,...,t_n)$.

Suppose first that k=1. If the unification algorithm finds a substitution $\{x_1/r_1\}$, say, which unifies $p(s_1,...,s_n)$ and $p(t_1,...,t_n)$, then equality axiom 5 can be used to show that $\forall((s_1=t_1)\wedge...\wedge(s_n=t_n)\rightarrow(x_1=r_1))$ is a logical consequence of the equality theory. Otherwise, we use equality axiom 5 and one of the equality axioms 1 to 4 to conclude that $\sim\exists((s_1=t_1)\wedge...\wedge(s_n=t_n))$ is a logical consequence of the equality theory.

Suppose now that the result holds for k-1. Let $p(s_1,...,s_n)$ and $p(t_1,...,t_n)$ be such that it takes the unification algorithm k steps to show that they are unifiable or not. Suppose that $\theta_1 = \{x_1/r_1'\}$ is the first substitution made by the unification algorithm. Hence $p(s_1,...,s_n)\theta_1$ and $p(t_1,...,t_n)\theta_1$ are such that the unification algorithm can discover in k-1 steps whether they are unifiable or not.

Suppose that $p(s_1,...,s_n)\theta_1$ and $p(t_1,...,t_n)\theta_1$ are not unifiable. Then the induction hypothesis gives that $\sim\exists((s_1=t_1)\theta_1\wedge...\wedge(s_n=t_n)\theta_1)$ is a logical consequence of the equality theory. It then follows from this and the fact that θ_1 was the first substitution made by the unification algorithm that

On the other hand, suppose that $p(s_1,...,s_n)\theta_1$ and $p(t_1,...,t_n)\theta_1$ are unifiable. Then the induction hypothesis gives that $\forall((s_1=t_1)\theta_1\wedge...\wedge(s_n=t_n)\theta_1\rightarrow(x_2=r_2)\wedge...\wedge(x_k=r_k))$ is a logical consequence of the equality theory. It follows from this, the fact that r_1 is $r_1'\gamma$, where $\gamma = \{x_2/r_2,...,x_k/r_k\}$, and equality axioms 6, 7 and 8 that $\forall((s_1=t_1)\wedge...\wedge(s_n=t_n)\rightarrow(x_1=r_1)\wedge...\wedge(x_k=r_k))$ is a logical consequence of the equality theory ∎

Lemma 15.2 Let P be a general program and G a general goal. Suppose the selected literal in G is positive.

(a) If there are no derived goals, then G is a logical consequence of comp(P).

(b) If the set $\{G_1,...,G_r\}$ of derived goals is non-empty, then $G\leftrightarrow G_1\wedge...\wedge G_r$ is a logical consequence of comp(P).

Proof Suppose G is the general goal $\leftarrow M_1,...,M_q$ and the selected positive literal M_i is $p(s_1,...,s_n)$. If the completed definition for p is $\forall(\sim p(x_1,...,x_n))$, then it is clear that G is a logical consequence of comp(P).

Next suppose that the completed definition of p is

$$\forall(p(x_1,...,x_n)\leftrightarrow E_1\vee...\vee E_k)$$

where E_i is

$$\exists y_1...\exists y_{d_i}\ ((x_1=t_{i,1})\wedge...\wedge(x_n=t_{i,n})\wedge L_{i,1}\wedge...\wedge L_{i,m_i})$$

It follows that

$$G \leftrightarrow$$

$$\wedge_{i=1}^{k} \sim\exists(M_1\wedge...\wedge M_{i-1}\wedge(s_1=t_{i,1})\wedge...\wedge(s_n=t_{i,n})\wedge L_{i,1}\wedge...\wedge L_{i,m_i}\wedge M_{i+1}\wedge...\wedge M_q)$$

is a logical consequence of comp(P). If $p(s_1,...,s_n)$ does not unify with the head of any general program clause in the definition of p, then it follows from lemma 15.1(a) that G is a logical consequence of comp(P).

On the other hand, suppose θ is an mgu of $p(s_1,...,s_n)$ and $p(t_{i,1},...,t_{i,n})$. Then we have that

$$\exists(M_1\wedge...\wedge M_{i-1}\wedge(s_1=t_{i,1})\wedge...\wedge(s_n=t_{i,n})\wedge L_{i,1}\wedge...\wedge L_{i,m_i}\wedge M_{i+1}\wedge...\wedge M_q) \leftrightarrow$$
$$\exists((M_1\wedge...\wedge M_{i-1}\wedge L_{i,1}\wedge...\wedge L_{i,m_i}\wedge M_{i+1}\wedge...\wedge M_q)\theta)$$

is a logical consequence of comp(P), using lemma 15.1(b) and the equality axioms 6, 7 and 8. Thus, if $\{G_1,...,G_r\}$ is the set of derived goals, then $G\leftrightarrow G_1\wedge...\wedge G_r$ is a logical consequence of comp(P) ∎

The next result is due to Clark [10].

Theorem 15.3 (Soundness of the negation as failure rule)

Let P be a general program, G a general goal and R a safe computation rule. If P ∪ {G} has a finitely failed SLDNF-tree via R, then G is a logical consequence of comp(P).

Proof The proof is by induction on the number n of (successful and unsuccessful) negative subgoals selected during the construction of the finitely failed tree (including the attempted construction of any subsidiary finitely failed trees).

Suppose first that n=0. Then the result follows by a straightforward induction on the depth of the tree, using lemma 15.2.

Next suppose the result holds for k<n. Consider a finitely failed SLDNF-tree for P ∪ {G}, whose construction requires the selection of n negative subgoals. There must be at least one goal, whose selected literal is negative, appearing on this tree. Choose a goal $\leftarrow M_1,...,M_q$ of least depth in this tree whose selected literal is negative. By repeated applications of lemma 15.2 and using the induction hypothesis, it suffices to show that $\sim\exists(M_1\wedge...\wedge M_q)$ is a logical consequence of comp(P). Suppose that the selected literal M_i is ~A, where $A\in B_P$. There are two cases to consider.

(a) ~A succeeds.

Thus ~A is deleted from $\leftarrow M_1,...,M_q$. By the induction hypothesis, $\sim\exists(M_1\wedge...\wedge M_{i-1}\wedge M_{i+1}\wedge...\wedge M_q)$ is a logical consequence of comp(P). Hence $\sim\exists(M_1\wedge...\wedge M_q)$ is also a logical consequence of comp(P).

(b) ~A fails.

This means that there is an SLDNF-refutation of ←A. Now recall that for a goal whose selected literal is positive, the derived goal is a logical consequence of the given goal and the input clause. Thus, using proposition 14.1 and applying the induction hypothesis on any (successful) negative subgoals in this refutation, we obtain that A is a logical consequence of comp(P). Hence $\sim\exists(M_1\wedge...\wedge M_q)$ is also a logical consequence of comp(P). (This last step uses the fact that A is ground) ∎

Corollary 15.4 Let P be a program. If $A\in F_P$, then ~A is a logical consequence of comp(P).

Now we come to the soundness of SLDNF-resolution. This result, which generalizes theorem 7.1, is essentially due to Clark [10].

Theorem 15.5 (Soundness of SLDNF-resolution)

Let P be a general program, G a general goal and R a safe computation rule. Then every R-computed answer substitution for $P \cup \{G\}$ is a correct answer substitution for $comp(P) \cup \{G\}$.

Proof Let G be the general goal $\leftarrow L_1,...,L_k$ and $\theta_1,...,\theta_n$ be the sequence of mgu's used in an SLDNF-refutation of $P \cup \{G\}$ via R. We have to show that $\forall((L_1 \wedge ... \wedge L_k)\theta_1...\theta_n)$ is a logical consequence of comp(P). The result is proved by induction on the length of the SLDNF-refutation.

Suppose first that n=1. This means that G has the form $\leftarrow L_1$. We consider two cases.

(a) L_1 is positive.

Thus P has a unit clause of the form $A\leftarrow$ and $L_1\theta_1 = A\theta_1$. Since $L_1\theta_1$ is an instance of a unit clause of P, it follows that $\forall(L_1\theta_1)$ is a logical consequence of P and, hence, comp(P).

(b) L_1 is negative.

In this case, L_1 is ground, θ_1 is the identity substitution and theorem 15.3 shows that L_1 is a logical consequence of comp(P).

Next suppose that the result holds for R-computed answer substitutions which come from SLDNF-refutations of length n–1. Suppose $\theta_1,...,\theta_n$ is the sequence of mgu's used in the SLDNF-refutation of $P \cup \{G\}$ of length n. Let L_m be the selected literal of G. We consider two cases.

(a) L_m is positive.

Let $A\leftarrow M_1,...,M_q$ $(q \geq 0)$ be the first input clause. By the induction hypothesis, $\forall((L_1 \wedge ... \wedge L_{m-1} \wedge M_1 \wedge ... \wedge M_q \wedge L_{m+1} \wedge ... \wedge L_k)\theta_1...\theta_n)$ is a logical consequence of comp(P). Thus, if $q>0$, $\forall((M_1 \wedge ... \wedge M_q)\theta_1...\theta_n)$ is a logical consequence of comp(P). Consequently, $\forall(L_m\theta_1...\theta_n) = \forall(A\theta_1...\theta_n)$ is a logical consequence of comp(P). Hence we have that $\forall((L_1 \wedge ... \wedge L_k)\theta_1...\theta_n)$ is a logical consequence of comp(P).

(b) L_m is negative.

In this case, L_m is ground, θ_1 is the identity substitution and theorem 15.3 shows that L_m is a logical consequence of comp(P). Using the induction hypothesis, we thus obtain that $\forall((L_1 \wedge ... \wedge L_k)\theta_1...\theta_n)$ is a logical consequence of comp(P) ∎

Finally, we turn to the problem of lifting the restriction that computation rules be safe. First we show that we cannot simply drop the condition in theorem 15.3 that R be safe.

Example Consider the general program P

$p(a) \leftarrow \sim q(x)$

$q(a) \leftarrow$

Let R be any unsafe computation rule, which allows negative subgoals to proceed even if they are not ground. Then $\leftarrow p(a)$ has a finitely failed SLDNF-tree via R. The subgoal $\sim q(x)$ fails because there is a refutation of $\leftarrow q(x)$ in which x is bound to a. However, it is easy to see that $\sim p(a)$ is not a logical consequence of comp(P).

It is possible to weaken the safeness condition a little and still obtain the results. Consider the class of computation rules with the following property. Non-ground negative subgoals are allowed to proceed. If the negative subgoal succeeds, then we proceed as before. However, if the negative subgoal fails, a check is made to make sure no bindings were made to any variables in the top-level goal of the corresponding refutation. If no such binding was made, then the negative subgoal is allowed to fail and we proceed as before. But, if such a binding *was* made, then the negative subgoal is delayed in the hope that more of its variables will be bound later. Alternatively, a control error could be generated and the program halted.

The key point here is that the refutation which causes the negative subgoal to fail must prove something of the form $\forall(A)$ rather than only $\exists(A)$. For this class of computation rules, theorems 15.3 and 15.5 continue to hold. The only change to their proofs is in the very last step in the proof of theorem 15.3.

The simplest way to implement a safe computation rule in a PROLOG system is to delay negative subgoals until any variables appearing in the subgoal have been bound to ground terms. For example, this is the method used by MU-PROLOG [45]. Unfortunately, the majority of PROLOG systems do not have a mechanism for delaying subgoals and so this solution is not available to them. Worse still, most PROLOG systems do not bother to check that negative subgoals are ground when called. This can lead to rather bizarre behaviour.

p(a) ←

q(b) ←

and the general goal ← ~p(x),q(x). If this program and goal are run on a PROLOG system which uses the standard computation rule and does not bother to check that negative subgoals are ground when called, then it will return the answer "no"! On the other hand, MU-PROLOG will delay the first subgoal, solve the second subgoal and then solve the first subgoal to give the correct answer {x/b}. Of course, the problem with this particular goal can be fixed for a standard PROLOG system by reordering the subgoals in the goal. However, that is not the point. A problem similar to this could lie undetected deep inside a very large and complex software system.

§16. COMPLETENESS OF THE NEGATION AS FAILURE RULE

In this section, we prove that, in the setting of programs and goals, the converse of theorem 15.3 holds. We also present a summary of the main results of the chapter.

The next result is due to Jaffar, Lassez and Lloyd [29]. The simpler definition of the equivalence relation in the proof, which avoids most of the technical complications of the original proof in [29], is due to Wolfram, Maher and Lassez [58].

Theorem 16.1 (Completeness of the negation as failure rule)

Let P be a program, G a goal and R a fair computation rule. If G is a logical consequence of comp(P), then P ∪ {G} has a finitely failed SLD-tree via R.

Proof Let G be the goal $\leftarrow A_1,\ldots,A_q$. Suppose that P ∪ {G} does not have a finitely failed SLD-tree via R. We prove that comp(P) ∪ $\{\exists(A_1\wedge\ldots\wedge A_q)\}$ has a model.

Let BR be any non-failed branch in the SLD-tree for P ∪ {G} via R. Suppose BR is G_0=G, G_1,... with mgu's θ_1, θ_2,... and input clauses C_1, C_2,.... The first step is to use BR to define a pre-interpretation J for P.

Suppose L is the underlying first order language for P. Naturally, L is assumed to be rich enough to support any standardizing apart necessary in BR. We define a relation * on the set of all terms in L as follows. Let s and t be terms in L. Then s*t if there exists $n \geq 1$ such that $s\theta_1...\theta_n = t\theta_1...\theta_n$, that is, $\theta_1...\theta_n$ unifies s and t. It is clear that * is indeed an equivalence relation. We then define the domain D of the pre-interpretation J as the set of all *-equivalence classes of terms in L. If s is a term in L, we denote the equivalence class containing s by [s].

Next we give the assignment of the constants and functions in L. If c is a constant in L, we assign c to [c]. If f is an n-ary function in L, we assign to f the function from D^n into D defined by $([s_1],...,[s_n]) \rightarrow [f(s_1,...,s_n)]$. It is clear that the function is indeed well-defined. This completes the definition of J.

The next task is to give the assignment of the predicates in order to extend J to an interpretation for comp(P) ∪ $\{\exists(A_1 \wedge ... \wedge A_q)\}$. For this purpose, we define the set I_0 as follows:

$$I_0 = \{p([t_1],...,[t_n]) : p(t_1,...,t_n) \text{ appears in BR}\}.$$

We show that $I_0 \subseteq T_P^J(I_0)$, where T_P^J is the mapping associated with the pre-interpretation J. Suppose that $p([t_1],...,[t_n]) \in I_0$, where $p(t_1,...,t_n)$ appears in some G_i, $i \in \omega$. Because R is fair and because BR is not failed, there exists $j \in \omega$ such that $p(s_1,...,s_n) = p(t_1,...,t_n)\theta_{i+1}...\theta_{i+j}$ appears in goal G_{i+j} and $p(s_1,...,s_n)$ is the selected atom in G_{i+j}. Suppose C_{i+j+1} is $p(r_1,...,r_n) \leftarrow B_1,...,B_m$. By the definition of T_P^J, it follows that $p([r_1\theta_{i+j+1}],...,[r_n\theta_{i+j+1}]) \in T_P^J(I_0)$. Then, using the fact that $\theta_1...\theta_k$ is idempotent, for each k, we have that

$$\begin{aligned} & p([t_1],...,[t_n]) \\ &= p([t_1\theta_{i+1}...\theta_{i+j}],...,[t_n\theta_{i+1}...\theta_{i+j}]) \\ &= p([s_1],...,[s_n]) \\ &= p([s_1\theta_{i+j+1}],...,[s_n\theta_{i+j+1}]) \\ &= p([r_1\theta_{i+j+1}],...,[r_n\theta_{i+j+1}]), \end{aligned}$$

so that $p([t_1],...,[t_n]) \in T_P^J(I_0)$. Thus $I_0 \subseteq T_P^J(I_0)$.

Now, by proposition 5.2, there exists I such that $I_0 \subseteq I$ and $I = T_P^J(I)$. I gives the assignments of the predicates in L. We assign = to the identity relation on D.

This completes the definition of the interpretation I, together with = assigned the identity relation, for comp(P) ∪ $\{\exists(A_1 \wedge ... \wedge A_q)\}$. Note that this interpretation is a model for $\exists(A_1 \wedge ... \wedge A_q)$ because $I_0 \subseteq I$. Note further that this interpretation is clearly a model for the equality theory. Hence, proposition 14.3 gives that I, together with = assigned the identity relation, is

Corollary 16.2 Let P be a program and $A \in B_P$. If $\sim$A is a logical consequence of comp(P), then $A \in F_P$.

The model constructed in the proof of theorem 16.1 is not a Herbrand model. In fact, the next example shows that theorem 16.1 simply cannot be proved by restricting attention to Herbrand models.

Example Consider the program P

p(f(y)) ← p(y)

q(a) ← p(y)

Note that $q(a) \notin F_P$. Now $gfp(T_P)=\emptyset$ and hence $q(a) \notin gfp(T_P)$. According to proposition 14.7, comp(P) ∪ {q(a)} does not have a Herbrand model.

The following example shows that unfortunately we cannot extend theorem 16.1 to arbitrary general programs.

Example Consider the general program P

q(a) ← ~r(a)

r(a) ← p(a)

r(a) ← ~p(a)

p(x) ← p(f(x))

Then it is easy to show that ~q(a) is a logical consequence of comp(P), but that P ∪ {←q(a)} does not have a finitely failed SLDNF-tree, for any computation rule.

Next, we turn to the question of completeness of SLDNF-resolution.

Example Consider the program

p(x) ←

q(a) ←

r(b) ←

and the goal ←p(x),~q(x). Clearly, x/b is a correct answer substitution. However, this answer substitution can never be computed, nor can any more general version of it.

This simple example clearly illustrates one of the problems in obtaining a completeness result for SLDNF-resolution. SLD-resolution returns most general answers. In the above example, it will return ϵ for the subgoal p(x). What we would like is for the negation as failure rule to now further instantiate x by the binding x/b and go on to compute the correct answer. However, negation as failure is only a test and cannot make any bindings. Unless it is presented with a goal which already is the root of a finitely failed SLD-tree, it has no machinery for further instantiating the goal so as to obtain such a tree. In the above example, ←q(x) is not the root of a finitely failed SLD-tree and negation as failure has no way to find the appropriate binding x/b.

The example shows that even restrictions such as only allowing correct answer substitutions which make the negative literals ground and requiring each variable which appears in a negative literal to also appear in a positive literal are not strong enough to force completeness. Even stronger restrictions on either the correct answer substitution or the program are required.

The next example illustrates another problem in obtaining a completeness result for SLDNF-resolution.

Example Consider the general program P

r(a) ← p(a)

r(a) ← ~p(a)

p(x) ← p(f(x))

Then the identity substitution ϵ is a correct answer substitution for comp(P) ∪ {←r(a)}, but ϵ cannot be R-computed, for any computation rule R.

The completeness of the negation as failure rule and SLDNF-resolution are of such importance that finding some form of completeness result for general programs and general goals is an urgent priority. A result along these lines appears in [10], but the condition required (the "hierarchical constraint") is too strong to be useful.

Finally, we summarize the main results for programs given in this chapter. First we need one more definition. The *Herbrand rule* is that if comp(P) ∪ {A} has no Herbrand model, then infer ~A.

We now have three possible rules for inferring negative information: the CWA, the Herbrand rule and the negation as failure rule. Then we have the following results in which P is a program (see Figure 6):

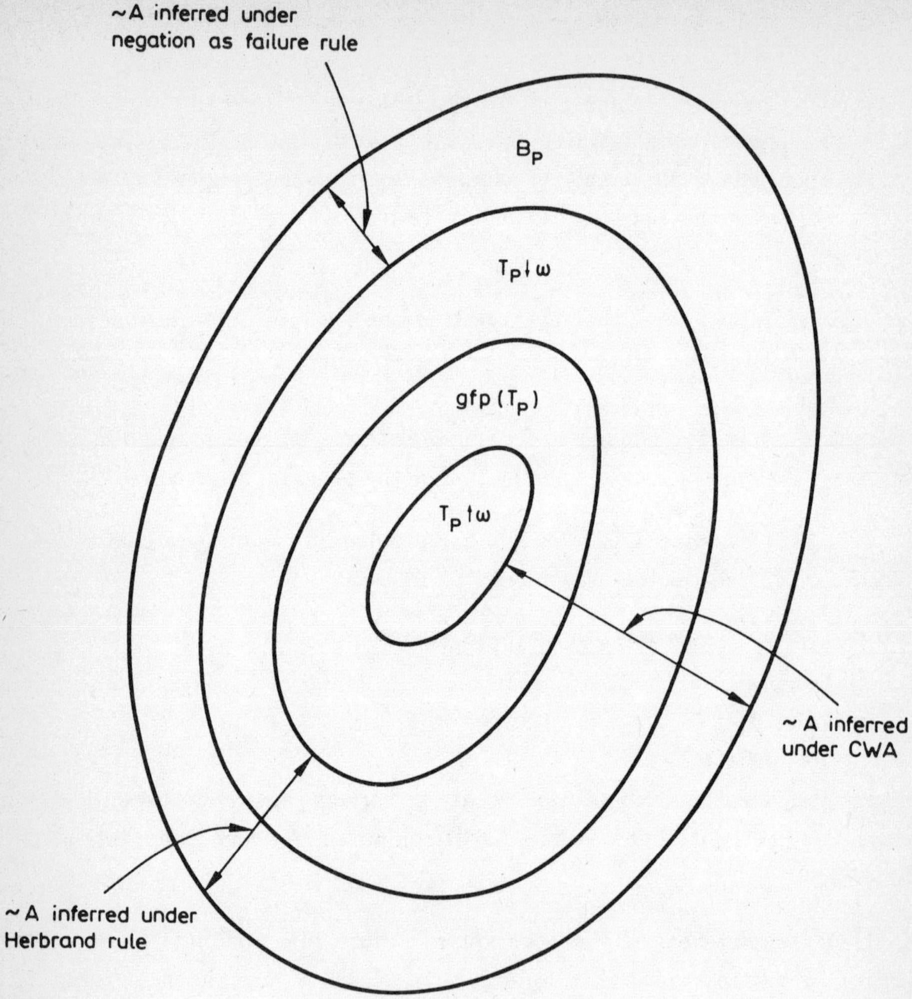

Fig. 6. Relationship between the various rules

$\{A \in B_P : \sim A \text{ can be inferred under the negation as failure rule}\} = B_P \backslash T_P \downarrow \omega$
$\{A \in B_P : \sim A \text{ can be inferred under the Herbrand rule}\} = B_P \backslash gfp(T_P)$
$\{A \in B_P : \sim A \text{ can be inferred under the CWA}\} = B_P \backslash T_P \uparrow \omega$
Since we have $T_P \uparrow \omega \subseteq gfp(T_P) \subseteq T_P \downarrow \omega$, it follows that the CWA is the most powerful rule, followed by the Herbrand rule, followed by the negation as failure rule. Since $T_P \uparrow \omega$, $gfp(T_P)$ and $T_P \downarrow \omega$ are generally distinct (see problem 12, chapter 1), it follows that the rules are distinct.

We can combine theorem 13.6 and corollaries 15.4 and 16.2.

Theorem 16.3 Let P be a program and $A \in B_P$. Then the following are equivalent:
(a) $A \in F_P$.
(b) $A \notin T_P \downarrow \omega$.
(c) A is in the SLD finite failure set.
(d) For every fair computation rule R, the corresponding SLD-tree for $P \cup \{\leftarrow A\}$ via R is finitely failed.
(e) $\sim A$ is a logical consequence of comp(P).

We can also combine theorems 15.3 and 16.1.

Theorem 16.4 Let P be a program and G a goal. Then G is a logical consequence of comp(P) iff $P \cup \{G\}$ has a finitely failed SLD-tree.

It is also worth emphasizing the following facts, which highlight the difference between (arbitrary) models and Herbrand models for comp(P) and between $T_P \downarrow \omega$ and $gfp(T_P)$. Let $A \in B_P$. Then we have
(a) $A \in gfp(T_P)$ iff $comp(P) \cup \{A\}$ has a Herbrand model.
(b) $A \in T_P \downarrow \omega$ iff $comp(P) \cup \{A\}$ has a model.

PROBLEMS FOR CHAPTER 3

1. Let P be a program. Show that $F_P^d = B_P \backslash T_P \downarrow d$, for $d \geq 1$.

2. Prove lemma 13.2.

3. Prove lemma 13.3.

4. Show that the converse of proposition 13.4 does not hold. In fact, show that, given k, there exists a program P and $A \in B_P$ such that $A \notin T_P \downarrow 2$ and yet the depth of every SLD-tree for $P \cup \{\leftarrow A\}$ is at least k.

5. Let P be a program and G a goal. Then G is called *infinite* (with respect to P) if for every computation rule R, the corresponding SLD-tree for $P \cup \{G\}$ via R is infinite. Show that there exists a program P and $A \in B_P$ such that $\leftarrow A$ is infinite and A is in the success set of P.

6. Let P be a program, $A \in B_P$ and A not be in the success set of P. Show that $\leftarrow A$ is infinite iff A is not in the SLD finite failure set.

7. Consider the program P

p(x) ← q(y), r(y)
q(h(y)) ← q(y)
r(g(y)) ←

Find two computation rules, one which leads to an infinite SLD-tree for $P \cup \{\leftarrow p(a)\}$ and one which leads to a finitely failed SLD-tree.

8. Extend the definition of T_P to general programs and show that T_P may then no longer be monotonic. Show that comp(P) may not be consistent, if P is a general program.

9. Use equality axioms 6 and 8 to show that = is an equivalence relation.

10. Let P be a general program and $s,t \in U_P$. Prove the following:
(a) s=s is a logical consequence of the equality theory.
(b) If s and t are syntactically different, then $s \neq t$ is a logical consequence of the equality theory.
(c) The domain of every model for comp(P) contains an isomorphic copy of U_P and =, restricted to U_P, is the identity relation.

11. Prove proposition 14.2.

12. Show that proposition 14.4 does not hold for general programs.

13. Show that corollary 15.4 no longer holds if we drop any one of the equality axioms 1 to 5 from the definition of comp(P).

14. Show that the condition that R be safe cannot be dropped from theorem 15.5.

15. Consider the general program P

$p(a) \leftarrow \sim q(x)$
$q(a) \leftarrow$

Show that $\sim p(a)$ is not a logical consequence of comp(P).

16. Consider the general program P

$p(a) \leftarrow \sim r(a)$
$r(a) \leftarrow q(x)$
$q(a) \leftarrow$

Show that, using any computation rule R, the goal $\leftarrow p(a)$ has a finitely failed SLDNF-tree via R and that $\sim p(a)$ is a logical consequence of comp(P). This program looks equivalent to the one in problem 15. Explain the difference.

17. Consider the program P

$p(f(y)) \leftarrow p(y)$
$q(a) \leftarrow p(y)$

and let A be q(a). Calculate the model for comp(P) $\cup$ {A} that would be given by the construction in theorem 16.1 for this program. Show that the domain of the model is isomorphic to $U_P \cup Z$, where Z is the integers.

18. Consider the general program P

$q(a) \leftarrow \sim r(a)$
$r(a) \leftarrow p(a)$
$r(a) \leftarrow \sim p(a)$
$p(x) \leftarrow p(f(x))$

Show that $\sim q(a)$ is a logical consequence of comp(P), but that $P \cup \{\leftarrow q(a)\}$ does not have a finitely failed SLDNF-tree, for any computation rule.

19. Consider the general program P

$r(a) \leftarrow p(a)$

$r(a) \leftarrow \sim p(a)$

$p(x) \leftarrow p(f(x))$

Show that the identity substitution ϵ is a correct answer substitution for comp(P) ∪ {←r(a)}, but that ϵ cannot be R-computed, for any computation rule R.

Chapter 4. PERPETUAL PROCESSES

A perpetual process is a program which does not terminate and yet is doing useful computation, in some sense. With the advent of PROLOG systems for concurrent applications [11], [12], [54], especially operating systems, more and more programs will be of this type. Unfortunately, the semantics for logic programs developed in chapters 1 and 2 does not apply to perpetual processes, simply because they do not terminate. Starting from the pioneering work of Andreka, van Emden, Nemeti and Tiuryn [1], we discuss in this chapter the basic results of a semantics for perpetual processes.

§17. COMPLETE HERBRAND INTERPRETATIONS

In this section, we introduce complete Herbrand interpretations. We define the complete Herbrand universe and base and prove that they are compact metric spaces under a suitable metric. Some elementary notions from metric space topology, all of which can be found in [17], will be required.

The complete Herbrand universe for a program is the collection of all (possibly infinite) terms which can be constructed from the constants and functions in the program. Thus our first task is to give a precise definition of a (possibly infinite) term, which extends the definition given in §2 of a (finite) term.

Let ω^* denote the set of all finite lists of non-negative integers. Lists are denoted by $[i_1,\ldots,i_k]$, where $i_1,\ldots,i_k \in \omega$. If $m,n \in \omega^*$, then $[m,n]$ denotes the list which is the concatenation of m and n. If $n \in \omega^*$ and $i \in \omega$, then $[n,i]$ denotes the list $[n,[i]]$. We let $|X|$ denote the cardinality of a set X. Similarly, if $n \in \omega^*$, then $|n|$ denotes the number of elements of n.

Definition We say $T \subseteq \omega^*$ is a *tree* if the following conditions are satisfied:
(a) For all $n \in \omega^*$ and for all $i,j \in \omega$, we have $[n,i] \in T$ and $j < i$ implies $n \in T$ and $[n,j] \in T$.
(b) $|\{i : [n,i] \in T\}|$ is finite, for all $n \in T$.

Definition A tree T is *finite* if T is a finite subset of ω^*. Otherwise, T is *infinite.*

Example The finite tree {[], [0], [1], [2], [1,0], [1,1], [2,0], [2,1], [2,2]} can be pictured as in Figure 7.

The infinite tree {[], [0], [1], [1,0], [1,1], [1,1,0], [1,1,1], [1,1,1,0], [1,1,1,1],...} can be pictured as in Figure 8.

Intuitively, each $n \in T$ is a node of the tree T. Condition (b) in the definition of tree states that each node has bounded degree.

We let S be a set of *symbols* and ar be a mapping from S into ω, which determines the *arity* of each symbol in S.

Definition A *term (over S)* is a function $t : dom(t) \rightarrow S$ such that
(a) The domain of t, dom(t), is a non-empty tree.
(b) For all $n \in dom(t)$, $ar(t(n)) = |\{i : [n,i] \in dom(t)\}|$.

We say the tree dom(t) *underlies* t. We let $Term_S$ denote the set of all terms over S.

Intuitively, a term is a (possibly infinite) tree, whose nodes are labelled by symbols in such a way that the arity of the label of each node is equal to the degree of that node.

Definition The term t is *finite* if dom(t) is finite. Otherwise, t is *infinite.*

Definition Let t be a term. The *depth*, dp(t), of t is defined as follows:
(a) If t is infinite, then $dp(t) = \infty$.
(b) If t is finite, then $dp(t) = 1 + \max\{|n| : n \in dom(t)\}$.

It will be convenient to have available the concept of the *truncation at depth n* ($n \in \omega$) of a term t, denoted by $\alpha_n(t)$. For this purpose, we introduce a new symbol Ω of arity 0, which will be used to indicate that a branch of the term t has been cut off in the truncation. Thus α_n is a mapping from $Term_S$

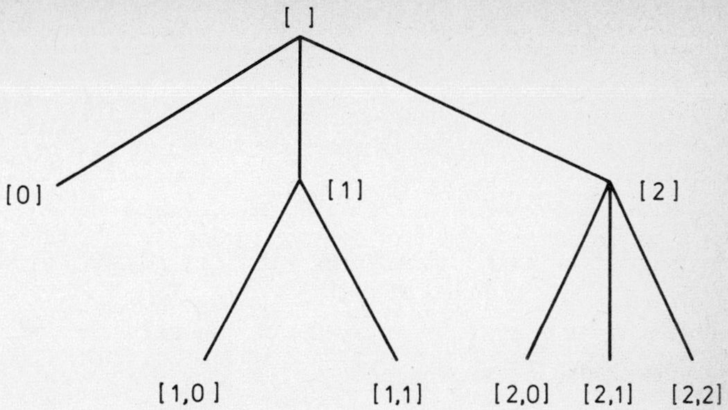

Fig. 7. A finite tree

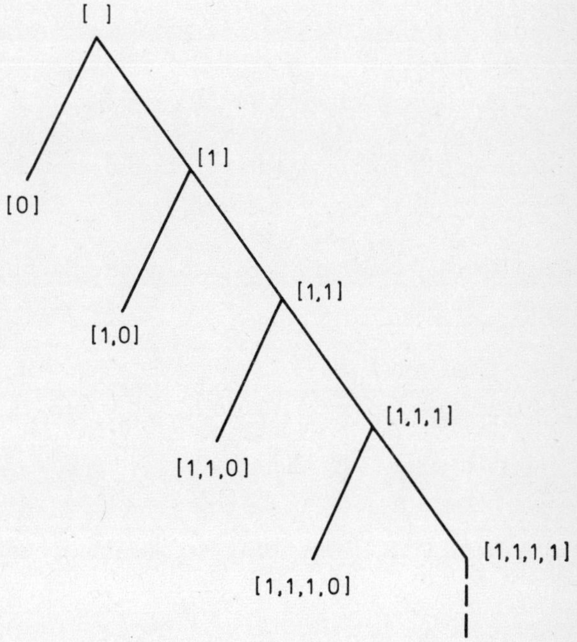

Fig. 8. An infinite tree

into $\mathrm{Term}_{S \cup \{\Omega\}}$ defined as follows:
(a) $\mathrm{dom}(\alpha_n(t)) = \{m \in \mathrm{dom}(t) : |m| \leq n\}$.
(b) $\alpha_n(t) : \mathrm{dom}(\alpha_n(t)) \rightarrow S \cup \{\Omega\}$ is defined by

$$\alpha_n(t)(m) = t(m), \quad \text{if } |m| < n$$
$$= \Omega, \quad \text{if } |m| = n.$$

Clearly, $\alpha_n(t)$ is a finite term with $\mathrm{dp}(\alpha_n(t)) \leq n+1$.

Term_S can be made into a metric space in a natural way. First, we recall the definition of a metric space [17].

Definition Let X be a set. A mapping $d : X \times X \rightarrow$ non-negative reals is a *metric* for X if
(a) $d(x,y) = 0$ iff $x=y$, for all $x,y \in X$.
(b) $d(x,y) = d(y,x)$, for all $x,y \in X$.
(c) $d(x,z) \leq d(x,y) + d(y,z)$, for all $x,y,z \in X$.
d is an *ultrametric* [3] if
(d) $d(x,z) \leq \max\{d(x,y), d(y,z)\}$, for all $x,y,z \in X$.

Definition (X,d) is a *metric space*, if d is a metric on X. If d is an ultrametric, then (X,d) is an *ultrametric space*.

Ultrametric spaces have topological properties rather similar to discrete metric spaces [3].

Now let $s,t \in \mathrm{Term}_S$. If $s \neq t$, then it is clear that $\alpha_n(s) \neq \alpha_n(t)$, for some $n>0$. Consequently, if $s \neq t$, then $\{n : \alpha_n(s) \neq \alpha_n(t)\}$ is not empty. We define $\alpha(s,t) = \min\{n : \alpha_n(s) \neq \alpha_n(t)\}$. Thus $\alpha(s,t)$ is the least depth at which s and t differ.

Proposition 17.1 (Term_S, d) is an ultrametric space, where d is defined by

$$d(s,t) = 0, \quad \text{if } s=t$$
$$= 2^{-\alpha(s,t)}, \quad \text{otherwise.}$$

Proof Straightforward. (The details are left to problem 1) ∎

Convergence in the topology induced by d is denoted by $\rightarrow$. Thus $t_n \rightarrow t$ means that the sequence $\{t_n\}_{n \in \omega}$ converges to t in this topology. The closure of a set A in this topology is denoted by $\overline{A}$.

Definition A metric space (X,d) is *compact* if every sequence in X has a subsequence which converges to a point in X.

A crucial fact about $Term_S$ is given by the following well known proposition [44].

Proposition 17.2 ($Term_S$, d) is compact iff S is finite.

Proof Suppose first that S is infinite. Let $\{t_s : s \in S\}$ be any collection of terms with the property that $t_s([])=s$ (that is, the root is labelled by s). If $s_1 \neq s_2$, then $d(t_{s_1}, t_{s_2}) = 1/2$. Thus $Term_S$ is not compact.

Conversely, suppose that S is finite. Let $\{t_k\}_{k \in \omega}$ be a sequence in $Term_S$. We consider two cases.

(a) There exists $m \in \omega$ and $l \in \omega$ such that, for all $n \geq l$, we have $dp(t_n) \leq m$.
Since S is finite, there are only a finite number of terms over S of depth $\leq$ m. Hence $\{t_k\}_{k \in \omega}$ must have a constant and, hence, convergent subsequence.

(b) Given $m \in \omega$ and $l \in \omega$, there exists $n \geq l$ such that $dp(t_n) > m$.
In this case, we can suppose without loss of generality that the sequence $\{t_k\}_{k \in \omega}$ is such that $dp(t_k) > k$, for $k \in \omega$. Note that every subsequence of $\{t_k\}_{k \in \omega}$ has the property that the depths of the terms in the subsequence are unbounded.

We define by induction an infinite term $t \in Term_S$ such that, for each $n \geq 1$, there exists a subsequence $\{t_{k_m}\}_{m \in \omega}$ of $\{t_k\}_{k \in \omega}$ with $\alpha_n(t_{k_m}) = \alpha_n(t)$, for $m \in \omega$.

Suppose first that n=1. Since S is finite, a subsequence $\{t_{k_m}\}_{m \in \omega}$ of $\{t_k\}_{k \in \omega}$ must have the same symbol s labelling their root nodes. We define $t([]) = s$.

Next suppose that t is defined up to depth n. Thus there exists a subsequence $\{t_{k_m}\}_{m \in \omega}$ of $\{t_k\}_{k \in \omega}$ such that $\alpha_n(t_{k_m}) = \alpha_n(t)$, for $m \in \omega$. Since S is finite, there exists a subsequence $\{t_{k_{m_p}}\}_{p \in \omega}$ of $\{t_{k_m}\}_{m \in \omega}$ such that the $\alpha_{n+1}(t_{k_{m_p}})$ are all equal, for $p \in \omega$. Define the nodes at depth n+1 for t in the same way as each of the $t_{k_{m_p}}$. This completes the inductive definition.

Since it is clear that t is an accumulation point of $\{t_k\}_{k \in \omega}$, we have

Now we are in a position to define the complete Herbrand universe. Let P be a program and F be the finite set of functions and constants in P. We regard constants as functions of arity 0.

Definition The *complete Herbrand universe* U_P' for P is $Term_F$. The elements of U_P' are called *ground terms.*

Thus U_P' is the set of all ground (possibly infinite) terms which can be formed out of the functions and constants appearing in P. It is straightforward to show that "ground term", as defined in §3, can be identified with "finite ground term", as just defined. This identification is taken for granted throughout this chapter. Thus we have $U_P \subseteq U_P'$. As long as P contains at least one function, it is clear that U_P is a proper subset of U_P'.

We adopt the convention throughout this chapter that "term", without qualification, will always mean a possibly infinite term. If a term is finite, this will always be explicitly stated.

Despite the fact that we have given a rather formal definition of term, in the material which follows we will rarely make direct reference to this definition, relying instead on the reader's intuitive understanding of a term. All the arguments presented could easily be formalized, if desired. We will also find it convenient to use a more informal notation for terms. In particular, for finite terms we will continue to use the old notation.

Example fff... is the infinite term pictured in Figure 9.
f(a,f(a,f(a,...))) is the infinite term pictured in Figure 10.

Proposition 17.3 Let P be a program. Then U_P' is a compact metric space, under the metric d introduced earlier.

Proof The result follows from proposition 17.2, since the set of functions and constants in P is finite ∎

The proof of the next result is straightforward.

Proposition 17.4 Let P be a program. Then U_P is dense in U_P', under the topology induced by d.

Fig. 9. The infinite term fff ...

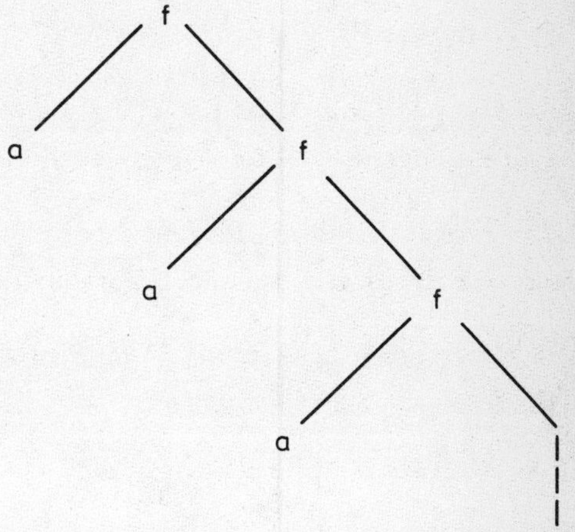

Fig. 10. The infinite term f(a,f(a,f(a,...)))

U'_P is called "complete" because it is the completion [17] of the metric space U_P. We will also require the concept of a (possibly infinite) atom. Let P be a program, F be the set of functions and constants in P, R be the set of predicates in P and V be the set of variables in P (more precisely, the first order language underlying P). All variables have arity 0.

Definition An *atom* A is an element of $Term_{V \cup F \cup R}$ such that $A(n) \in R$ iff $n=[]$, for all $n \in dom(A)$.

Thus an atom is a term with the root node (only) labelled by a predicate. In a similar way as for terms, we can identify "finite atom", as just defined, with "atom", as defined in §2. Whenever an atom is finite, this will always be explicitly stated in this chapter.

Definition The *complete Herbrand base* B'_P for a program P is the set of all terms A in $Term_{F \cup R}$ for which $A(n) \in R$ iff $n=[]$, for all $n \in dom(A)$. The elements of B'_P are called *ground atoms.*

Thus B'_P is the set of all ground (possibly infinite) atoms which can be formed out of the finite set of predicates, functions and constants appearing in P. Note that $B_P \subseteq B'_P$.

Proposition 17.5 Let P be a program. Then B'_P is a compact metric space, under the metric d introduced earlier.

Proof $Term_{F \cup R}$ is compact, by proposition 17.2. It is easy to show that B'_P is a closed and, therefore, compact subspace of $Term_{F \cup R}$ ∎

Proposition 17.6 Let P be a program. Then B_P is dense in B'_P, under the topology induced by d.

Proof Straightforward ∎

The concept of a substitution applied to an atom in §4 can be easily generalized to the more general definition of atom and term. We restrict attention to ground substitutions applied to finite atoms, which is all that is needed in this chapter.

Definition A *ground substitution* θ is a finite set of the form $\{v_1/t_1,\ldots,v_n/t_n\}$, where each v_i is a variable, the variables are distinct and $t_i \in U'_P$, for $i=1,\ldots,n$.

Definition Let A be a finite atom with variables $\{v_1,...,v_n\}$ and $\theta = \{v_1/t_1,...,v_n/t_n\}$ be a ground substitution. Then $A\theta$ is the ground atom defined as follows:

(a) $dom(A\theta) = dom(A) \cup \{[m,n] : m \in dom(A), A(m)=v_i$ and $n \in dom(t_i)$, for some $i \in \{1,...,n\}\}$.

(b) $A\theta : dom(A\theta) \to F \cup R$ is defined by

$A\theta(m) = A(m)$, if $m \in dom(A)$ and $A(m) \notin \{v_1,...,v_n\}$

$A\theta([m,n]) = t_i(n)$, if $m \in dom(A)$, $A(m)=v_i$ and $n \in dom(t_i)$, for some $i \in \{1,...,n\}$.

We say $A\theta$ is a *ground instance* of A. The collection of all ground instances of the finite atom A is denoted by [[A]]. Note that $[A] \subseteq [[A]] \subseteq B'_P$.

Proposition 17.7 Let P be a program and $C = \{A_1,...,A_m\}$ be a set of finite atoms with variables $x_1,...,x_n$. Consider the mapping

$$S_C : (U'_P)^n \to (B'_P)^m$$

defined by

$$S_C(t_1,...,t_n) = (A_1\theta,...,A_m\theta),$$

where $\theta = \{x_1/t_1,...,x_n/t_n\}$. Then S_C is continuous, where $(U'_P)^n$ and $(B'_P)^m$ are each given the product topology.

Proof Suppose that $\{(t_{1,k},...,t_{n,k})\}_{k\in\omega}$ converges to $(t_1,...,t_n)$ in the product topology on $(U'_P)^n$. Put $\theta_k = \{x_1/t_{1,k},...,x_n/t_{n,k}\}$, for $k \in \omega$. Clearly $A_i\theta_k \to A_i\theta$, for i=1,...,m, and hence S_C is continuous ∎

Proposition 17.8 Let A be a finite atom. Then [[A]] is a closed subset of B'_P.

Proof Put $C = \{A\}$. If A has n variables, then $[[A]] = S_C((U'_P)^n)$. Since S_C is continuous and U'_P is compact, $S_C((U'_P)^n)$ is a compact and, therefore, closed subset of B'_P ∎

Proposition 17.9 Let A be a finite atom. Then $\overline{[A]} = [[A]]$.

Proof Since $[A] \subseteq [[A]]$ and [[A]] is closed, $\overline{[A]} \subseteq [[A]]$. On the other hand, if C={A} and A has n variables, then $[[A]] = S_C((U'_P)^n) = S_C((\overline{U_P})^n) \subseteq \overline{S_C((U_P)^n)} = \overline{[A]}$, by propositions 17.4 and 17.7 ∎

We conclude this section with the definition of a complete Herbrand interpretation and the mapping T'_P.

Definition Let P be a program. An interpretation for P is a *complete Herbrand interpretation* if the following conditions are satisfied:
(a) The domain of the interpretation is the complete Herbrand universe U'_P.
(b) Constants in P are assigned to "themselves" in U'_P.
(c) If f is an n-ary function in P, then f is assigned to the mapping from $(U'_P)^n$ into U'_P defined by $(t_1,...,t_n) \rightarrow f(t_1,...,t_n)$.

We make no restrictions on the assignment of the predicates in P, so that different complete Herbrand interpretations arise by taking different such assignments. In an analogous way to §3, we identify a complete Herbrand interpretation with a subset of B'_P. The set of all complete Herbrand interpretations for P is a complete lattice under the partial order of set inclusion.

Definition A *complete Herbrand model* for P is a complete Herbrand interpretation which is a model for P.

We also define a mapping T'_P from the lattice of complete Herbrand interpretations to itself as follows. Let I be a complete Herbrand interpretation. Then $T'_P(I) = \{A \in B'_P : A \leftarrow B_1,...,B_n$ is a ground instance of a clause in P and $\{B_1,...,B_n\} \subseteq I\}$.

Note that T'_P is T^J_P for the pre-interpretation J consisting of the domain U'_P and the above assignments of constants and functions. It turns out that because of the compactness of U'_P and B'_P, T'_P has an even richer set of properties than T_P. We explore these properties in the next section.

§18. PROPERTIES OF T'_P

In this section we establish various important properties of T'_P, notably that $gfp(T'_P) = T'_P \downarrow \omega$.

We begin with four results, which are the analogues for T'_P of propositions 6.1, 6.3 and 6.4 and theorem 6.5. The proofs of these results are essentially the same as the earlier ones.

Proposition 18.1 (Model intersection property)

Let P be a program and $\{M_i\}_{i\in I}$ be a non-empty set of complete Herbrand models for P. Then $\cap_{i\in I} M_i$ is a complete Herbrand model for P.

We let M'_P denote the least complete Herbrand model for P, which is the intersection of all complete Herbrand models for P.

Proposition 18.2 Let P be a program. Then the mapping T'_P is continuous (in the lattice-theoretic sense of §5) and, hence, monotonic.

Proposition 18.3 Let P be a program and I be a complete Herbrand interpretation for P. Then I is a model for P iff $T'_P(I) \subseteq I$.

Theorem 18.4 Let P be a program. Then $M'_P = \text{lfp}(T'_P) = T'_P\uparrow\omega$.

The next result appeared in [1].

Theorem 18.5 (Closedness of T'_P)

Let P be a program and I be a closed subset of B'_P. Then $T'_P(I)$ is a closed subset of B'_P. Furthermore, $\overline{T'_P(J)} \subseteq T'_P(\overline{J})$, for $J \subseteq B'_P$.

Proof Let I be a closed subset of B'_P. We show $T'_P(I)$ is closed. We can immediately reduce to the case when P consists of a single clause, say, $A\leftarrow A_1,\ldots,A_m$. Suppose the clause has n variables. Put $C=\{A, A_1,\ldots,A_m\}$ and let S_C be the associated mapping defined in §17. Since S_C is continuous and U'_P is compact, we have that $S_C((U'_P)^n)$ is a closed subset of $(B'_P)^{m+1}$. Let π denote the projection from $(B'_P)^{m+1}$ onto its first component. Then $T'_P(I) = \pi(S_C((U'_P)^n) \cap (B'_P \times I^m))$ and thus $T'_P(I)$ is closed.

For the last part, it is straightforward to show that T'_P maps closed sets to closed sets iff $\overline{T'_P(J)} \subseteq T'_P(\overline{J})$, for $J \subseteq B'_P$ ∎

Corollary 18.6 $T'_P\downarrow k$ is closed, for $k\in\omega$. Furthermore, $T'_P\downarrow\omega$ is closed.

Note carefully that we do not necessarily have the opposite inclusion $\overline{T'_P(J)} \supseteq T'_P(\overline{J})$, for $J \subseteq B'_P$.

Example Let P be the program

q(a) ← p(f(x),f(x))

Let $J = \{p(t,f(t)) : t\in U_P\}$. Then $T'_P(\overline{J})=\{q(a)\}$, but $\overline{T'_P(J)}=\emptyset$.

we need the concept of the limit superior of a sequence of subsets of a metric space [3].

Definition Let (X,d) be a metric space and $\{Y_n\}_{n\in\omega}$ be a sequence of subsets of X. Then we define $LS_{n\in\omega}(Y_n) = \{x\in X :$ for every neighbourhood V of x and for every $m\in\omega$, there exists $k\geq m$ such that $V\cap Y_k\neq\emptyset\}$.

If $\{Y_n\}_{n\in\omega}$ is a decreasing sequence of closed sets, it is easy to show that $LS_{n\in\omega}(Y_n)=\cap_{n\in\omega}Y_n$.

Theorem 18.7 (Weak continuity of T_P')

Let P be a program and $\{I_k\}_{k\in\omega}$ be a sequence of sets in B_P'. Then $LS_{k\in\omega}(T_P'(I_k)) \subseteq T_P'(LS_{k\in\omega}(I_k))$.

Proof Suppose $A\in LS_{k\in\omega}(T_P'(I_k))$. Then for every neighbourhood V of A, there exists infinitely many k such that $V\cap T_P'(I_k)\neq\emptyset$. Since P is finite, there exists a clause $A_0\leftarrow A_1,...,A_m$ in P, a subsequence $\{I_{k_l}\}_{l\in\omega}$ of $\{I_k\}_{k\in\omega}$ and a sequence $\{\theta_l\}_{l\in\omega}$ of ground substitutions for the variables $x_1,...,x_n$ of the clause such that $A_0\theta_l\to A$ and $A_j\theta_l\in I_{k_l}$, for j=1,...,m and $l\in\omega$.

Suppose θ_l is $\{x_1/t_{1,l},...,x_n/t_{n,l}\}$. Since U_P' is compact, we can assume without loss of generality that $(t_{1,l},...,t_{n,l})\to(t_1,...,t_n)$, say. Put $\theta = \{x_1/t_1,...,x_n/t_n\}$. By proposition 17.7, we have that $(A_0\theta_l,...,A_m\theta_l)\to(A_0\theta,...,A_m\theta)$. Since $A_0\theta_l\to A$, we have that $A_0\theta=A$. Furthermore, since $A_j\theta_l\to A_j\theta$, we have that $A_j\theta\in LS_{k\in\omega}(I_k)$, for j=1,...,m. Hence $A\in T_P'(LS_{k\in\omega}(I_k))$ ∎

Note that we do not generally have $LS_{k\in\omega}(T_P'(I_k)) = T_P'(LS_{k\in\omega}(I_k))$.

Example Consider the program

q(a) ← p(f(x),f(x))

Put $I_k=\{p(f^k(a),f^{k+1}(a))\}$, for $k\in\omega$. Then $LS_{k\in\omega}(I_k)=\{p(fff...,fff...)\}$. Thus $T_P'(LS_{k\in\omega}(I_k))=\{q(a)\}$, but $LS_{k\in\omega}(T_P'(I_k))=\emptyset$.

Corollary 18.8 (Intersection property for T_P')

Let P be a program and $\{I_k\}_{k\in\omega}$ be a decreasing sequence of closed sets in B_P'. Then $T_P'(\cap_{k\in\omega}I_k) = \cap_{k\in\omega}T_P'(I_k)$.

Proof We have that

$T'_P(\cap_{k\in\omega} I_k)$

$= T'_P(LS_{k\in\omega}(I_k))$, since I_k are closed and decreasing

$\supseteq LS_{k\in\omega}(T'_P(I_k))$, by theorem 18.7

$= \cap_{k\in\omega} T'_P(I_k)$, since $T'_P(I_k)$ are closed and decreasing.

Furthermore, since T'_P is monotonic, we have $T'_P(\cap_{k\in\omega} I_k) \subseteq \cap_{k\in\omega} T'_P(I_k)$

∎

We cannot drop the requirement that each I_k be closed in corollary 18.8.

Example Consider the program

$q(a) \leftarrow p(f(x))$

Let I_k be $\{p(f^n(a)) : n \geq k\}$, for $k\in\omega$. Then $\{I_k\}_{k\in\omega}$ is a decreasing sequence. Furthermore, $\cap_{k\in\omega} I_k = \emptyset$, so that $T'_P(\cap_{k\in\omega} I_k) = \emptyset$. However, $T'_P(I_k) = \{q(a)\}$, for $k\in\omega$. Thus $\cap_{k\in\omega} T'_P(I_k) = \{q(a)\}$.

Part (a) of the next theorem is due to Andreka, van Emden, Nemeti and Tiuryn [1]. Recall that it can happen that $gfp(T_P) \neq T_P\downarrow\omega$.

Theorem 18.9 Let P be a program. Then we have

(a) $gfp(T'_P) = T'_P\downarrow\omega$.

(b) $T'_P(\cap_{k\in\omega} \overline{T_P\downarrow k}) \supseteq \cap_{k\in\omega} \overline{T_P\downarrow k}$.

Proof (a) It suffices to show that $T'_P(T'_P\downarrow\omega) = T'_P\downarrow\omega$. Now we have

$T'_P(T'_P\downarrow\omega)$

$= T'_P(\cap_{k\in\omega} T'_P\downarrow k)$

$= \cap_{k\in\omega} T'_P(T'_P\downarrow k)$, by corollaries 18.6 and 18.8

$= T'_P\downarrow\omega$.

(b) We have

$T'_P(\cap_{k\in\omega} \overline{T_P\downarrow k})$

$\supseteq \cap_{k\in\omega} \overline{T'_P(T_P\downarrow k)}$, by theorem 18.5

$\supseteq \cap_{k\in\omega} \overline{T_P\downarrow k}$ ∎

It is apparent that the essential reason that $gfp(T'_P)=T'_P\downarrow\omega$ is because U'_P is compact. We generally have $gfp(T_P)\neq T_P\downarrow\omega$ precisely because limits of sequences of finite terms are missing from U_P. In many respects, T'_P, U'_P and B'_P give a more appropriate setting for the foundations of logic programming than T_P, U_P and B_P.

Note that $\cap_{k\in\omega} \overline{T_P\downarrow k}$ may not be a fixpoint of T'_P.

Example Let P be the program

q(a) ← p(x,f(x))

p(f(x),f(x)) ← p(x,x)

Then $\cap_{k\in\omega} \overline{T_P\downarrow k}$ = {p(fff...,fff...)}, but $T'_P(\cap_{k\in\omega} \overline{T_P\downarrow k})$ = {q(a), p(fff...,fff...)}.

Proposition 18.10 Let P be a program. Then we have

(a) $\overline{T_P\downarrow k} = T'_P\downarrow k$, for k=0, 1.

(b) $\overline{T_P\downarrow k} \subseteq T'_P\downarrow k$, for k≥2.

Proof By corollary 18.6, $T'_P\downarrow k$ is closed, for $k\in\omega$. Also it is easy to show by induction that $T_P\downarrow k \subseteq T'_P\downarrow k$, for $k\in\omega$. Thus we have $\overline{T_P\downarrow k} \subseteq T'_P\downarrow k$, for $k\in\omega$. Furthermore, $\overline{T_P\downarrow 0} = \overline{B_P} = B'_P = T'_P\downarrow 0$. Finally, we leave the proof that $\overline{T_P\downarrow 1} = T'_P\downarrow 1$ to problem 9 ∎

Note that $\overline{T_P\downarrow k}$ may be a proper subset of $T'_P\downarrow k$, for k≥2 (see problem 10).

Proposition 18.11 Let P be a program. Then $\overline{T_P\downarrow\omega} \subseteq \cap_{k\in\omega} \overline{T_P\downarrow k} \subseteq T'_P\downarrow\omega$.

Proof We have

$\overline{T_P\downarrow\omega}$

$= \overline{\cap_{k\in\omega} T_P\downarrow k}$

$\subseteq \cap_{k\in\omega} \overline{T_P\downarrow k}$

$\subseteq \cap_{k\in\omega} T'_P\downarrow k$, by proposition 18.10

$= T'_P\downarrow\omega$ ∎

Note that both of the inclusions of proposition 18.11 may be proper (see problem 11).

Finally, we prove a useful characterization of $\cap_{k\in\omega}\overline{T_P\downarrow k}$.

Theorem 18.12 Let P be a program and $A\in B'_P$. Then the following are equivalent:

(a) $A\in \cap_{k\in\omega}\overline{T_P\downarrow k}$.

(b) There exists a sequence $\{A_k\}_{k\in\omega}$ such that $A_k\in T_P\downarrow k$, for $k\in\omega$, and $A_k\rightarrow A$.

(c) There exists a finite atom B and a non-failed fair derivation $\leftarrow B=G_0$, G_1,... with mgu's θ_1, θ_2,... such that $A\in \cap_{k\in\omega}[[B\theta_1...\theta_k]]$. (If the derivation is successful, then the intersection is over the finite set of non-negative integers which index the goals of the derivation).

Proof The equivalence of (a) and (b) is left to problem 12.

(c) implies (a). Suppose (c) holds. By proposition 17.9, we have that $A\in \cap_{n\in\omega}\overline{[B\theta_1...\theta_n]}$. By proposition 13.5, given $k\in\omega$, there exists $n\in\omega$ such that $[B\theta_1...\theta_n] \subseteq T_P\downarrow k$. Hence $A\in \cap_{k\in\omega}\overline{T_P\downarrow k}$.

(b) implies (c). For this proof, we let R denote the computation rule which always chooses the leftmost atom in a goal, but puts the introduced atoms at the *end* of the derived goal. R is clearly a fair computation rule.

Let $\{A_k\}_{k\in\omega}$ be a sequence such that $A_k\in T_P\downarrow k$, for $k\in\omega$, and $A_k\rightarrow A$. Since $A_k\in T_P\downarrow k$, proposition 13.4 shows that there is a derivation D_k via R beginning with $\leftarrow A_k$, which is either successful (that is, D_k is a refutation of $P\cup\{\leftarrow A_k\}$) or has length $>$ k. We consider two cases.

(1) Given $m\in\omega$ and $l\in\omega$, there exists $n\geq l$ such that D_n has length $>$ m.

In this case, by passing to an appropriate subsequence, we can assume without loss of generality that the sequence $\{A_k\}_{k\in\omega}$ is such that $A_k\in T_P\downarrow k$,

We now prove by induction that there exists a finite atom B and an infinite derivation $\leftarrow B=G_0, G_1,\ldots$ via R with input clauses $C_1, C_2,\ldots$ such that, for each $n\in\omega$, there exists a subsequence $\{A_{k_m}\}_{m\in\omega}$ of $\{A_k\}_{k\in\omega}$, where $C_1,\ldots,C_{n+1}$ are the same (up to variants) as the first n+1 input clauses of each of the D_{k_m} and G_{n+1} is more general than the (n+1)th goal in D_{k_m}, for $m\in\omega$.

Suppose first that n=0. Since P contains only finitely many clauses, a subsequence $\{A_{k_m}\}_{m\in\omega}$ of $\{A_k\}_{k\in\omega}$ must use the same program clause, say E, in the first step of D_{k_m}. We let B be the head of E and let C_1 be a suitable variant of E.

Next suppose the result holds for n–1. Thus there exists a finite atom B and a derivation $\leftarrow B=G_0, G_1,\ldots,G_n$ via R with input clauses $C_1,\ldots,C_n$ such that there exists a subsequence $\{A_{k_m}\}_{m\in\omega}$ of $\{A_k\}_{k\in\omega}$, where $C_1,\ldots,C_n$ are the same (up to variants) as the first n input clauses of each of the D_{k_m} and G_n is more general than the nth goal in D_{k_m}, for $m\in\omega$. Note that as the lengths of the D_{k_m} are unbounded, the nth goal in each D_{k_m} is not empty. Furthermore, the atom selected in the nth goal of each D_{k_m} is the first atom. Since P contains only finitely many clauses, a subsequence $\{A_{k_{m_p}}\}_{p\in\omega}$ of $\{A_{k_m}\}_{m\in\omega}$ must use the same program clause, say F, as the (n+1)th input clause of the derivation $D_{k_{m_p}}$. It is clear that (a suitable variant of) F can be used as C_{n+1}. This completes the induction argument.

To finish off case (1), we have only to show that if $\theta_1, \theta_2,\ldots$ are the mgu's of the derivation just constructed, then $A\in[[B\theta_1\ldots\theta_n]]$, for $n\in\omega$. However, this follows from proposition 17.9, since, given $n\in\omega$, there exists a subsequence $\{A_{k_m}\}_{m\in\omega}$ such that $A_{k_m}\rightarrow A$ and $A_{k_m}\in[B\theta_1\ldots\theta_n]$. Thus A satisfies condition (c).

(2) There exists $m\in\omega$ and $l\in\omega$ such that, for all $n\geq l$, D_n has length $\leq$ m.

In this case, since each D_k is either successful or has length $> k$, we may assume without loss of generality that there exists $m \in \omega$ such that the sequence $\{A_k\}_{k \in \omega}$ has the properties that $A_k \rightarrow A$ and each D_k is successful with length $\leq m$. Because P is finite, there exists a subsequence $\{A_{k_m}\}_{m \in \omega}$ such that all the D_{k_m} have exactly the same sequence of input clauses (up to variants). Suppose E is the program clause used first in each of the D_{k_m}. We let B be the head of E and construct a refutation of $P \cup \{\leftarrow B\}$ of length $\leq m$ using the same sequence of input clauses as each of the D_{k_m}. In a similar way to case (1), we can show that A satisfies condition (c) ∎

§19. SEMANTICS OF PERPETUAL PROCESSES

As we stated above, a perpetual process is a program which does not terminate and yet is doing useful computation, in some sense. The problem is to find the appropriate sense of an infinite computation being "useful". We solve this problem by introducing the concept of an infinite atom in B'_P being "computable at infinity". The set of all such atoms plays the role for perpetual processes that the success set plays for programs which terminate. The major result of this section is that the set of all atoms computable at infinity is a subset of $\text{gfp}(T'_P)$.

We begin with the key definition.

Definition Let P be a program and $A \in B'_P \setminus B_P$. We say A is *computable at infinity* if there is a finite atom B and an infinite fair derivation $\leftarrow B = G_0$, $G_1, \ldots$ with mgu's $\theta_1, \theta_2, \ldots$ such that $d(A, B\theta_1 \ldots \theta_k) \rightarrow 0$, as $k \rightarrow \infty$.

We put $C_P = \{A \in B'_P \setminus B_P : A \text{ is computable at infinity}\}$.

Example Let P be the program

p(f(x)) ← p(x)

Since $\text{lfp}(T_P) = \emptyset$, this program does not compute anything in the sense of chapter 2. However, given the goal ←p(x), the atom p(fff...) can be "computed at infinity". In fact, it is clear that $C_P = \{p(fff\ldots)\}$.

Example Let P be the program

fib(x) ← fib1(0.1.x)

fib1(x.y.z.w) ← plus(x,y,z), fib1(y.z.w)

plus(0,x,x) ←

plus(f(x),y,f(z)) ← plus(x,y,z)

(Recall the convention that n stands for $f^n(0)$). Clearly fib(1.2.3.5.8.13....)$\in C_P$, where the argument of fib is the Fibonacci sequence. We simply let B be fib(x) and we obtain the approximating sequence fib(1.x_1), fib(1.2.x_2), fib(1.2.3.x_3),....

Example We consider Hamming's problem, which is to construct the sorted sequence t of positive integers containing no prime factors other than 2, 3 or 5. Thus the initial part of the sequence t is 2.3.4.5.6.8.9.10.12.15.... The following program P to solve this problem appeared in [11] and [24].

hamming(x) ← seqprod(1.x,2,u), seqprod(1.x,3,v), seqprod(1.x,5,w),
merge(u,v,z), merge(z,w,x)

merge(x.u,y.v,x.w) ← y>x, merge(u,y.v,w)

merge(x.u,y.v,y.w) ← x>y, merge(x.u,v,w)

merge(x.u,x.v,x.w) ← merge(u,v,w)

seqprod(x.u,y,z.v) ← prod(x,y,z), seqprod(u,y,v)

f(x)>f(y) ← x>y

f(x)>0 ←

prod(x,0,0) ←

prod(x,f(y),z) ← prod(x,y,w), plus(w,x,z)

plus(0,x,x) ←

plus(f(x),y,f(z)) ← plus(x,y,z)

Then it is clear that hamming(t)$\in C_P$.

The next proposition gives a characterization of C_P independent of the metric d.

Proposition 19.1 Let P be a program and $A \in B'_P \backslash B_P$. Then $A \in C_P$ iff there is a finite atom B and an infinite fair derivation $\leftarrow B = G_0, G_1, \ldots$ with mgu's $\theta_1, \theta_2, \ldots$ such that $\cap_{k \in \omega} [[B\theta_1 \ldots \theta_k]] = \{A\}$.

Proof We have to show that $d(A, B\theta_1 \ldots \theta_k) \to 0$, as $k \to \infty$, iff $\cap_{k \in \omega} [[B\theta_1 \ldots \theta_k]] = \{A\}$.

We suppose first that $\cap_{k \in \omega} [[B\theta_1 \ldots \theta_k]] = \{A\}$. Let us assume that there exists $n \in \omega$ such that, for all $k \in \omega$, we have $\alpha_n(A) \neq \alpha_n(B\theta_1 \ldots \theta_k)$. Hence, for each $k \in \omega$, $\alpha_n(B\theta_1 \ldots \theta_k)$ must have at least one node labelled by a variable. Since $\alpha_n(A)$ is finite, it is clear that there exists a node in $\alpha_n(A)$ and there exists $m \in \omega$ such that, for $k \geq m$, the corresponding node in $B\theta_1 \ldots \theta_k$ is labelled by a variable. (The variable may depend on k). Consequently, $\cap_{k \in \omega}[[B\theta_1 \ldots \theta_k]]$ contains not just A, but infinitely many ground infinite atoms. Thus our original assumption is incorrect and hence, given $n \in \omega$, there exists $k \in \omega$ such that $\alpha_n(A) = \alpha_n(B\theta_1 \ldots \theta_k)$. Thus $d(A, B\theta_1 \ldots \theta_k) \rightarrow 0$, as $k \rightarrow \infty$.

Conversely, let us suppose that $d(A, B\theta_1 \ldots \theta_k) \rightarrow 0$, as $k \rightarrow \infty$. Since each $[[B\theta_1 \ldots \theta_k]]$ is closed and $\{[[B\theta_1 \ldots \theta_k]]\}_{k \in \omega}$ is decreasing, it is clear that $A \in \cap_{k \in \omega}[[B\theta_1 \ldots \theta_k]]$. Next suppose $A' \in \cap_{k \in \omega}[[B\theta_1 \ldots \theta_k]]$. Let $\epsilon > 0$ be given. Choose m such that $d(A, B\theta_1 \ldots \theta_m) < \epsilon$. Suppose $A' = B\theta_1 \ldots \theta_m \theta$, for some θ. Thus $d(A, A') = d(A, B\theta_1 \ldots \theta_m \theta) < \epsilon$. Since ϵ was arbitrary, we have that $d(A, A') = 0$ and hence $A = A'$. Thus $\cap_{k \in \omega}[[B\theta_1 \ldots \theta_k]] = \{A\}$ ∎

We could have adopted a weaker definition of C_P in which we simply demand that $A \in \cap_{k \in \omega}[[B\theta_1 \ldots \theta_k]]$. However, the following example shows that this weaker definition doesn't properly capture the notion of "computable at infinity".

Example Let P be the program

$p(f(x)) \leftarrow p(f(x))$

Under the weaker definition, we would have $p(fff\ldots) \in C_P$.

Now we come to the main result of this chapter, which is based on the results of Andreka, van Emden, Nemeti and Tiuryn [1] and Nait Abdallah and van Emden [47].

Theorem 19.2 (Soundness of SLD-resolution for infinite computations) Let P be a program. Then $C_P \subseteq gfp(T'_P)$.

Proof We have

C_P	
$\subseteq \cap_{k \in \omega} \overline{T_P \downarrow k}$,	by theorem 18.12 and proposition 19.1
$\subseteq T'_P \downarrow \omega$,	by proposition 18.11
$= gfp(T'_P)$,	by theorem 18.9 ∎

Theorem 19.2 is the analogue for perpetual processes of theorem 8.3,

infinite atoms, it follows from theorem 19.2 that $C_P \subseteq gfp(T'_P)\backslash B_P$. It would be pleasant if $C_P = gfp(T'_P)\backslash B_P$. However, as the following examples show, this cannot be achieved without some restrictions on P or modifications to the definitions of C_P and T'_P or both.

Example Let P be the program

p(f(x)) ←

Then p(fff...)$\in gfp(T'_P)\backslash B_P$, but p(fff...)$\notin C_P$.

Example Let P be the program

p(f(x)) ← p(f(x))

Then p(fff...)$\in gfp(T'_P)\backslash B_P$, but p(fff...)$\notin C_P$.

Example Let P be the program

p(x,f(x)) ← p(x,x)

Then p(fff...,fff...)$\in gfp(T'_P)\backslash B_P$, but p(fff...,fff...)$\notin C_P$. The problem here is that no matter what we choose for B, the computation will fail. Note that p(fff...,fff...)$\in gfp(T'_P)$, because T'_P does not respect the occur check.

In view of these developments, we propose the following setting for perpetual processes. The intended interpretation of a perpetual process P is $gfp(T'_P)$. This is indeed a model for P. $gfp(T'_P)$ is the analogue of the intended interpretation $lfp(T_P)$ for (ordinary) programs. C_P is then the analogue of the success set for programs. For programs, we get soundness and completeness, since $lfp(T_P)$ = success set. For perpetual processes, we only have the soundness result $C_P \subseteq gfp(T'_P)$. As we have seen, completeness cannot be achieved without further restrictions.

Taking a complete Herbrand model as the intended interpretation seems to be the simplest and most natural way of providing a semantics for perpetual processes. The results of this chapter suggest that $gfp(T'_P)$ should be the intended interpretation. However, $gfp(T'_P)$ generally contains infinite atoms which are not intuitively computable at infinity and thus we do not get completeness. For a rather different approach to this topic, we suggest the reader consult [19].

This chapter leaves many questions unanswered. Finding a satisfactory semantics for perpetual processes and for communication between concurrent processes is a current research problem. We believe that the appropriate setting in which to discuss such problems is the setting of U'_P, B'_P and T'_P and that the basic results presented in this chapter will play a central role in any satisfactory semantics.

PROBLEMS FOR CHAPTER 4

1. Prove proposition 17.1.

2. Prove that "finite ground term" as defined in §17 can be identified with "ground term" as defined in §3.

3. Prove that U_P is dense in U'_P.

4. Suppose $I \subseteq B'_P$ and $A \in B_P$. Prove that $A \in \bar{I}$ iff $A \in I$.

5. Find a program P and a complete Herbrand model I for P such that $\bar{I}$ is not a model for P.

6. Show that we cannot drop the requirement that the sequence $\{I_k\}_{k \in \omega}$ be decreasing in corollary 18.8.

7. The set of all non-empty closed subsets of B'_P can be made into a metric space using the Hausdorff metric ρ defined by $\rho(C,D)=\max\{h(C,D), h(D,C)\}$, where C and D are non-empty closed subsets of B'_P and $h(C,D)=\sup\{d(x,D) : x \in C\}$ (see [17]).
(a) Show that if $A,B \in B'_P$, then $\rho(\{A\},\{B\}) = d(A,B)$.
(b) Show that if $\{C_n\}_{n \in \omega}$ is a decreasing sequence of closed subsets of B'_P, then $\{C_n\}_{n \in \omega}$ is convergent in the topology induced by ρ and its limit is $\bigcap_{n \in \omega} C_n$.
(c) Restrict further attention to P such that $T'_P(\emptyset) \neq \emptyset$. This restriction and the fact that T'_P is closed imply that T'_P is a well-defined mapping from the metric space of non-empty closed subsets of B'_P into itself. Part (b) suggests that corollary 18.8 can be extended by proving that T'_P is continuous in the topology induced by ρ. Show that this conjecture is false.

8. Show that $\mathrm{gfp}(T'_P)$ may no longer be equal to $T'_P{\downarrow}\omega$ if the program P is allowed to consist of an infinite number of clauses with an infinite number of constants.

9. Prove that $\overline{T_P{\downarrow}1} = T'_P{\downarrow}1$.

10. Find a program P such that $\overline{T_P{\downarrow}2} \subset T'_P{\downarrow}2$.

11. Find a program P such that $\overline{T_P{\downarrow}\omega} \subset \bigcap_{k\in\omega}\overline{T_P{\downarrow}k} \subset T'_P{\downarrow}\omega$.

12. Prove that $A \in \bigcap_{k\in\omega}\overline{T_P{\downarrow}k}$ iff there is a sequence $\{A_k\}_{k\in\omega}$ such that $A_k \in T_P{\downarrow}k$, for $k\in\omega$, and $A_k \rightarrow A$.

13. Illustrate theorem 18.12 with the program

p(f(x)) ← p(x)

and with A = p(fff...).

REFERENCES

[1] Andreka, H., van Emden, M.H., Nemeti, I. and Tiuryn, J., Infinite-Term Semantics for Logic Programs, draft manuscript, 1983.

[2] Apt, K.R. and van Emden, M.H., Contributions to the Theory of Logic Programming, JACM, 29, 3(July 1982), 841-862.

[3] Arnold, A. and Nivat, M., The Metric Space of Infinite Trees: Algebraic and Topological Properties, Fundamenta Informatica, 3, 4(1980), 445-476.

[4] Battani, G. and Meloni, H., Interpreteur du Language de Programmation PROLOG, Groupe d'Intelligence Artificielle, Université d'Aix-Marseille, 1973.

[5] Bibel, W., Automated Theorem Proving, Vieweg, Braunschweig, 1982.

[6] Bobrow, D.G. (Ed.), Special Issue on Non-monotonic Logic, Artificial Intelligence, 13, 1980.

[7] Bowen, K.A., Programming with Full First-Order Logic, Machine Intelligence 10, 1982, 421-440.

[8] Chang, C.L. and Lee, R.C.T., Symbolic Logic and Mechanical Theorem Proving, Academic Press, New York, 1973.

[9] Clark, K.L., Predicate Logic as a Computational Formalism, Research Report 79/59, Department of Computing, Imperial College.

[10] Clark, K.L., Negation as Failure, in Logic and Databases, H. Gallaire and

[11] Clark, K.L. and Gregory, S., A Relational Language for Parallel Programming, Proc. ACM Conf. on Functional Programming Languages and Computer Architecture, 1981, 171-178.

[12] Clark, K.L. and Gregory, S., PARLOG: A Parallel Logic Programming Language, Research Report DOC 83/5, Dept. of Computing, Imperial College, 1983.

[13] Clark, K.L. and McCabe, F., The Control Facilities of IC-PROLOG, in Expert Systems in the Micro Electronic Age, D. Michie (Ed.), Edinburgh University Press, 122-149.

[14] Clark, K.L. and Tarnlund, S.-A., A First Order Theory of Data and Programs, Proc. IFIP 77, North-Holland, 939-944.

[15] Colmerauer, A., Kanoui, H., Roussel, P. and Pasero, R., Un Systeme de Communication Homme-Machine en Francais, Groupe de Recherche en Intelligence Artificielle, Université d'Aix-Marseille, 1973.

[16] Davis, M. and Putnam, H., A Computing Procedure for Quantification Theory, JACM, 7(1960), 201-215.

[17] Dugundji, J., Topology, Allyn and Bacon, Boston, 1966.

[18] van Emden, M.H. and Kowalski, R.A., The Semantics of Predicate Logic as a Programming Language, JACM, 23, 4 (Oct. 1976), 733-742.

[19] Falaschi, M., Levi, G. and Palamidessi, C., On the Fixed-Point Semantics of Horn Clauses with Infinite Terms, Proc. Logic Programming Workshop '83, Portugal, 1983, 474-484.

[20] Gallaire, H. and Minker, J. (Eds.), Logic and Databases, Plenum Press, New York, 1978.

[21] Gallaire, H., Minker, J. and Nicolas, J. (Eds.), Advances in Database Theory, vol. 1, Plenum Press, New York, 1981.

[22] Gilmore, P.C., A Proof Method for Quantification Theory, IBM J. Res. Develop. 4(1960), 28-35.

[23] Green, C., Applications of Theorem Proving to Problem Solving, IJCAI-69, Washington, 1969, 219-239.

[24] Hansson, A., Haridi, S. and Tarnlund S.-A., Properties of a Logic Programming Language, in Logic Programming, K.L. Clark and S.-A. Tarnlund (Eds.), Academic Press, 1982, 267-280.

[25] Haridi, S. and Sahlin, D., Evaluation of Logic Programs Based on Natural Deduction, TRITA-CS-8305 B, Royal Institute of Technology, Sweden, 1983.

[26] Hayes, P.J., Computation and Deduction, Proc. MFCS Conference, Czechoslovakian Academy of Sciences, 1973.

[27] Herbrand, J., Researches in the Theory of Demonstration, in From Frege to Godel: A Source Book in Mathematical Logic, 1879-1931, J. van Heijenoort (Ed.), Harvard University Press, Mass., 1967, 525-581.

[28] Hill, R., LUSH-Resolution and its Completeness, DCL Memo 78, Department of Artificial Intelligence, University of Edinburgh, 1974.

[29] Jaffar, J., Lassez, J.-L. and Lloyd J.W., Completeness of the Negation as Failure Rule, IJCAI-83, Karlsruhe, 1983, 500-506.

[30] Kowalski, R.A., Logic for Problem Solving, Elsevier North Holland, New York, 1979.

[31] Kowalski, R.A., Predicate Logic as a Programming Language, IFIP 74, 569-574.

[32] Kowalski, R.A., Algorithm = Logic + Control, CACM, 22, 7 (Jul. 1979), 424-436.

[33] Kowalski, R.A. and Kuehner, D., Linear Resolution with Selection

Function, Artificial Intelligence, 2(1971), 227-260.

[34] Lassez, J.-L. and Maher, M.J., Closures and Fairness in the Semantics of Programming Logic, Theoretical Computer Science, to appear.

[35] Lassez, J.-L. and Maher, M.J., Semantics of Logic Programs, Dept. of Computer Science, University of Melbourne, in preparation.

[36] Lassez, J.-L., Nguyen, V.L. and Sonenberg, E.A., Fixed Point Theorems and Semantics: A Folk Tale, IPL, 14, 3(May 1982), 112-116.

[37] Lloyd, J.W., An Introduction to Deductive Database Systems, Australian Computer Journal, 15, 2(May 1983), 52-57.

[38] Loveland, D.W., Automated Theorem Proving: A Logical Basis, North-Holland, New York, 1978.

[39] Manna, Z., Mathematical Theory of Computation, McGraw Hill, New York, 1974.

[40] Martelli, A. and Montanari, U., Unification in Linear Time and Space: A Structured Presentation, Nota Interna B76-16, Instituto di Elaborazione della Informazione, Pisa, 1976.

[41] Martelli, A. and Montanari, U., An Efficient Unification Algorithm, ACM Trans. on Programming Languages and Systems, 4, 2(April 1982), 258-282.

[42] Mendelson, E., Introduction to Mathematical Logic (2nd Ed.), Van Nostrand, Princeton, 1979.

[43] Mota-Oka, T. (Ed.), Fifth Generation Computer Systems, Proc. Int. Conf. on Fifth Generation Computer Systems, JIPDEC, North-Holland, 1982.

[44] Mycielski, J. and Taylor, W., A Compactification of the Algebra of Terms, Algebra Universalis, 6(1976), 159-163.

[45] Naish, L., An Introduction to MU-PROLOG, Technical Report 82/2, Dept. of Computer Science, University of Melbourne.

[46] Naish, L., Automatic Generation of Control for Logic Programs, The Journal of Logic Programming, to appear.

[47] Nait Abdallah, A. and van Emden, M.H., Algorithm Theory and Logic Programming, draft manuscript, 1983.

[48] Paterson, M.S. and Wegman, M.N., Linear Unification, J. of Computer and Systems Sci., 16(1978), 158-167.

[49] Plaisted, D.A., The Occur-Check Problem in PROLOG, Int. Symp. on Logic Programming, Atlantic City, 1984, 272-280.

[50] Prawitz, D., An Improved Proof Procedure, Theoria, 26(1960), 102-139.

[51] Robinson, J.A., A Machine-oriented Logic Based on the Resolution Principle, JACM, 12, 1 (Jan. 1965), 23-41.

[52] Robinson, J.A., Logic: Form and Function, Edinburgh University Press, 1979.

[53] Roussel, P., PROLOG: Manuel de Reference et d'Utilization, Groupe d'Intelligence Artificielle, Université d'Aix-Marseille, 1975.

[54] Shapiro, E.Y., A Subset of Concurrent PROLOG and its Interpreter, Technical Report TR-003, ICOT, Tokyo, 1983.

[55] Shapiro, E.Y. and Takeuchi, A., Object-Oriented Programming in Concurrent PROLOG, New Generation Computing, 1, 1(1983), 25-48.

[56] Shoenfield, J., Mathematical Logic, Addison-Wesley, Reading, Mass., 1967.

Pacific J. Math., 5 (1955), 285-309.

[58] Wolfram, D.A., Maher, M.J. and Lassez, J.-L., A Unified Treatment of Resolution Strategies for Logic Programs, Second International Logic Programming Conference, Uppsala, 1984, 263-276.

NOTATION

$\cap$ set intersection

$\cup$ set union

$\in$ membership of

$\subseteq$ improper subset

$\supseteq$ improper superset

$\subset$ subset of

$\supset$ superset of

$\leftarrow, \rightarrow$ implication

$\leftrightarrow$ equivalence

$\wedge$ and

$\vee$ or

$\sim$ negation

$\forall$ universal quantifier

$\exists$ existential quantifier

$\emptyset$ empty set

∞ infinity

$|X|$ cardinality of X

$X \backslash Y$ set difference

$X \times Y$ cartesian product

▮ end of proof

P logic program

$\forall(F)$ 7

$\exists(F)$ 7

L 12, 25

U_L 15

B_L 15

U_P 16

B_P 16

T_P 30

M_P 29

F_P^d 65

F_P 66

C_P 107

U_P' 96

B_P' 98

M_P' 101

T_P' 100

T_P^J 72

$A \leftarrow B_1,\ldots,B_n$ 8

$A \leftarrow$ 8

$\leftarrow B_1,\ldots,B_n$ 9

$A \leftarrow L_1,\ldots,L_n$ 68

INDEX